Where Eagles Soar

JAMIE BUCKINGHAM

KINGSWAY PUBLICATIONS

EASTBOURNE

ISBN 0 86065 097 9

Unless otherwise indicated, Scripture quotations are from
the Authorized Version of the Bible.

RSV = Revised Standard Version of the Bible,
copyright 1946, 1952, © 1971, 1973

TLB = The Living Bible, © Tyndale House Publishers 1971

NEB = New English Bible, © Oxford and Cambridge
University Presses 1961, 1970

Front cover photo: Zefa Picture Library

Printed in Great Britain for
KINGSWAY PUBLICATIONS LTD
1 St Anne's Road, Eastbourne, E. Sussex BN21 3UN by
Clays Ltd, St Ives plc

WHERE EAGLES SOAR

To my dear friend and first publisher
Dan Malachuk
who not only pushed me
out of the nest but belongs
to that rare fraternity of
those with ice on their
wings who dare ride the
mighty *ruach* of God—
soaring above the storms

Contents

Preface

The engine on my ancient Cessna airplane was purring as I took off from the little grass airstrip near our home in Melbourne, Florida, to fly to Augusta, Georgia. It was a cold, blustery February morning. Other than the noise from the engine and the whistle of the wind past the rattling windows, the cockpit was quiet. My antique radio had stopped working moments after takeoff. That didn't bother me. I never did trust radio navigation anyway, having learned to fly by the seat of my pants in an old Piper cub on a dirt runway. All I needed was a compass and a map to get me to my destination.

But over south Georgia the ceiling began to drop. I was forced to climb out "on top"—over the clouds. It was beautiful up there, and the flying was smooth. But without landmarks—and without any kind of radio navigation to guide me—I was in critical danger of getting lost. Even though my compass was reliable—inerrant, to use an orthodox word—it gave little help and was basically ineffective without visual contact with the ground. I could be blown miles off course and never know it.

Within minutes I had a distinct sensation that the plane was drifting eastward, out over the Atlantic Ocean. In fact, on one occasion I lined up the nose of the plane on a distant cloud and could actually "see" the plane turning toward Spain. Every instinct

11

said to apply the left rudder to keep from drifting out over the water. I yearned for some contact with the ground, even for some friendly voice through the speaker from a radar operator telling me where I was. It was not enough to know which direction I was *pointed*—the direction I was *moving* was the critical factor.

An hour later the clouds began to break. To my horror, I saw water below me. I began an immediate descent, hoping I would not meet someone else coming up through the same hole. Once again I found myself wishing for something more than my compass and basic instruments to give me guidance and direction. The need for "control" beyond my own was vital.

It was not until I broke through the bottom layer of clouds that I discovered the water I had seen was actually the Savannah River. I was off course about 15 miles, but to the left I could see the skyline of my destination and knew that Augusta's Bush Field was nearby.

After I landed and parked the plane on the apron, I was met by an agent from the Federal Aviation Authority who had been in the tower when I came in—sans radio.

"You caused quite a stir up there," he said kindly, "coming in without a radio. We've been watching you on radar for 20 minutes and tried to contact you for landing instructions."

"Sorry," I said. "Mine is broken. Besides, I never have trusted radios. As long as I got that blinking green light from the tower, I figured it was okay to land."

"Things are changing," the inspector said. "It used to be all a pilot needed was a compass and a map. Now aviation has speeded up. Planes are faster and there are a lot more of them in the air. If you're going to fly into a controlled air space—get a good radio."

He paused. "In fact," he said, "I'm not going to let you take off without special permission. Call the tower on the phone when you're ready to leave, and then come out and wait in your plane. They'll signal you with the light when it's clear to taxi."

Then he added, "And don't come back to Bush Field until you have a functioning radio. This is controlled air space."

For a number of years I committed myself to the Bible as my compass in life. The radio of the Holy Spirit was a nuisance. It could not be trusted. Especially inaccurate, I thought, were messages from those who claimed to have various "gifts" of the Spirit. I preferred to fly by the seat of my pants—good old carnal sense—and stick to the Bible as my sole guide in life.

Now comes additional revelation, oddly, from the Bible itself. The Bible is not enough. In fact, it is ineffective and may even lead you astray unless it is interpreted by the Holy Spirit. I am not talking about "extra-Biblical" revelation. I am simply saying that if the Holy Spirit does not bring life to the written Word, the Bible at best is nothing more than beautiful literature. At worst it is bondage—producing legalism. Jesus, as reflected in John's Gospel, and Paul in his letters to the new Christian churches have much to say about this.

The Bible is known as the *logos*—the written word. But there is another word, equally important, known as the *rhema*. This is the "now word" of God to each individual. It is what brings the Bible alive. It is what makes the Bible meaningful to each individual life. It is the word of the Holy Spirit.

To say all a Christian needs is the Bible is an orthodox-evangelical fallacy which has been fostered upon us by generations of people who feared we might be pulled off course if we listened to the voice of the Holy Spirit. The Christian needs to check every voice against the Bible's infallible direction. But to live by the Bible alone means your doctrinal nose could be pointing true north while your entire life is moving out over the ocean. You'll never realize how critical your situation is until you run out of gas and have to ditch at sea—or you're hit from behind by a jet liner full of singing charismatics.

My friend, Bernie May, has a twin-engine Beechcraft that is full of sophisticated radio gear. Several weeks ago he flew down from his home in Waxhaw, North Carolina, and picked up our family to fly us back north for a skiing weekend. We left Melbourne early in the morning in a driving rain and were in rain, fog and severe turbulence all the way to our destination. But flying in bad weather is no problem to Bernie—because of all those navigation aids. He took his direction from the tower, found his course on his compass, climbed to his assigned altitude and set the automatic

13

pilot. From that point on, the radio—and the compass, working together—flew us safely to our destination.

That's what this book is all about. Balance. And the joy—and the risk—of the Spirit-controlled life. It is a book about the necessary venture—often tough, sometimes joyful, always fulfilling—that the believer must take to reach that life beyond his own control. The life in the Spirit.

JAMIE BUCKINGHAM
Melbourne, Florida

Where Eagles Soar

I

The Breath of God

"Watch the eagle," our Israeli guide said, pointing high above the Sinai desert at the silent figure, soaring close to the mountains. "He locks his wings, picks the thermals and rides the breath of God above the storm."

I was on a research trip in the Sinai Peninsula, collecting material for a book on the wilderness experience. For seven days our small group of men had been trekking the desert sand, making our way through the awesome wadis (dried riverbeds) and climbing the rugged stone mountains in the footsteps of Moses. Now we had reached Jebel Musa, the Mountain of Moses. Struggling in the darkness, we had climbed the backside of Mount Sinai to reach the summit by dawn. Now we were on our descent, following the steep path downward toward St. Catherine's Monastery, nestled far below against the base of the huge mountain.

It was then we spotted the eagle.

A huge storm, one of those rare phenomena of the desert, had built up over the Gulf of Suez and was now moving inland. The mighty thunderheads towered around 30,000 feet. It was awesome to behold as it moved to the south of us across the triangular-shaped peninsula toward Saudi Arabia where it would doubtless dissipate.

But it was the eagle which drew the attention of our guide. We were near the summit of the 7,600-foot mountain, and the eagle was already 10,000 feet above us. And climbing.

"That's what the prophet meant when he said God's people would mount up with wings as eagles," the tough, dark-skinned Israeli said as he squatted on the pathway, waiting for the rest of the men to catch up. I squatted down beside him, Bedouin fashion, and together we watched the eagle confront the massive storm clouds.

"How high will he go?" I asked.

"Over the storm. Twenty-five, thirty thousand feet. He is now beyond his own control. He locks his wings, here," he said—pointing at his shoulders—"and rides the wind of God."

Again he used that magnificent Hebrew word *ruach* to describe the thermals of the desert. It was the same word King David used in Psalm 51 to describe the Holy Spirit—the breath of God. "Take not thy *ruach* from me."

In the New Testament the word is softer, more gentle. There we find the Greek word *pneuma*, meaning breath or spirit. It is the same word from which we get "pneumatic." In the New Testament it is often used to describe a filling experience. So the Holy Spirit fills, much as one would blow air into a balloon. The thought is one of lifting—from within. But in the Old Testament, the Spirit of God, the *ruach*, is anything but gentle. Here it is a roaring wind, howling through the canyons and moaning over the mountains. It is the mighty winds of the storms blowing across the wilderness accompanied by flashing lightning and rumbling thunder. It is the hot air thermals rushing upward. And upon it rides the eagle, ascending to unbelievable heights, using the air currents which destroy things on the ground to carry him over the fury of the storm to safety on the other side.

I watched, fascinated, as the eagle circled and ascended until he was but a tiny dot against the onrushing storm. Then he disappeared altogether.

"He fears nothing," the guide said as we rose to greet the other men coming down the steep path. "Even though we no longer see him, he can see us. He can see for 50 miles. He will go so high he will be covered with ice—his head, his wings, everything Then he descends on the backside of the storm and the ice melts. Who knows, if it were not for the ice, he might just keep going up, touch God and never come down."

Our guide grinned, stretched and padded off barefooted down the rocky mountain trail.

It's interesting how I keep thinking of that eagle—and the breath of God upon which he rides. I think of him when storm clouds approach. I think of him when it seems I'm being swept, beyond control, to some dizzy encounter. I think of his determination, in the face of impossible odds, to lock his wings so that nothing can deter him from his upward climb. I think of him, even now, as I start work on this book.

It has been a dozen years since I had that exhilarating experience the Bible describes as the baptism in the Holy Spirit. I wrote about that experience, and the many lessons learned from it, in my earlier book *Risky Living*. For a while I was able to stay spiritually airborne on the enthusiasm alone. "Enthusiasm," by the way, comes from two Greek words, *en theos*, meaning "in God." But if the Christian walk is mere enthusiasm, we become nothing more than spiritual grasshoppers, going up and down but never learning how to soar. I need more than being "in God"; I must have God in me. Once airborne, I need some power to keep me aloft.

It was then I discovered there was more to the Christian life than living on experiences. Being born again is an experience. Being healed is an experience. Being baptized in the Holy Spirit is an experience. But if the experience does not open the door to an ongoing process, then we soon fall to earth again—battered, flattened, and often in worse shape than when we made our upward leap.

Conversion—turning your back on a self-centered way of life and allowing Jesus Christ to take total control—is an experience. But a man needs more than conversion, he needs salvation, which is an ongoing process. Salvation, in its truest sense, is becoming who we really are. And that process is never complete—at least not here on this earth.

Healing is an experience, and I am so grateful that thousands

19

of people are experiencing divine healing in their bodies. I am grateful the healing ministry is once again being recognized by the church as a valid experience. I am grateful that in liturgical and evangelical churches alike, men and women are discovering that one of the purposes of the redemption was not only to save us from sin but to save us from sickness. The same Jesus who healed 2,000 years ago is alive and, through His Holy Spirit, still healing bodies. But while divine healing is an experience, it is not enough. The people of God must move upward to the ongoing process of divine health. And that, like the process of salvation, demands discipline, exercise, determination and the supernatural power of the Holy Spirit.

Thus, when we come to the ministry of the Holy Spirit—as we will in this book—we find the same concepts. The baptism in the Holy Spirit is an experience. For many of us it was an exhilarating, revolutionary experience. It opened our eyes to understand the Bible. It was the instrument which allowed us to call Jesus lord in all areas of our lives. It brought freedom from the bondage of legalism and set in motion the various charismatic gifts which had laid dormant ever since the Holy Spirit first entered at conversion. But while the baptism in the Holy Spirit is an experience, the Spirit-controlled life is an ongoing process. It consists not only of allowing the breath of God *(pneuma)* to fill and expand you to the proper size and shape, but it consists of allowing the wind of God *(ruach)* to bear you aloft—and keep you there. The *ruach* not only controls your path of flight in the face of oncoming storms, but He enables you to soar the exalted corridors of heaven and brush your wings against the face of God.

There are certain things you must do, however, before that is possible. For one, you must recognize who you are. You are an eagle, not a grasshopper. Then you must be willing to cooperate with God, to put yourself in takeoff position for God to fill—and send you soaring. To remain on your nest when the storm blows is disastrous. Your only hope is to launch out in faith against all insurmountable obstacles, lock your wings and let God do the rest

That's the reason I'm writing this book. To take you with me on some of my own flights (and some of my mountain-smashing experiences). I am writing to encourage you to soar like the eagle: be filled with the Holy Spirit and ride the wind of God.

II

Dealing
with the Awful Sins

For two months I had this particular week scheduled on my calendar to lay aside everything else and finish work on this book. Yet it seemed the world was not going to turn me loose. All week long I have been bombarded with intense, exhausting situations—situations which have forced me to relive much of my own dark past. And though I am no longer ashamed to uncover these black pits of my personal history when I see similar traits emerging in the lives of others I deeply love, their vicarious suffering is almost as bad as the actual pain of personal experience.

It has been a week during which the lid has been pulled back on the lives of three other ministers—all friends of mine—to reveal the murky shadows of adulterous relationships. As if by divine design they have come to us at this particular time, writhing and suffering in the same fires I've been through. And I've found myself virtually helpless to do anything but love and pray.

Our stories are not pleasant. I tell them to illustrate our mutual need to get beyond ourselves, beyond our own control and into the searing light of holy exposure where we can at last discover the comfort of knowing our lives are lived completely through the Spirit's guidance.

One of my closest friends is the former pastor of a large denominational church. Four months ago he called on the phone. He was being forced to leave his church. For some time he had been involved with another woman in an extra-marital relationship. It had been discovered and his kingdom had fallen around him.

Such disclosure should not shock or dismay Christians, for ministers—even Spirit-baptized ministers—are no less susceptible to the surging drives of sex and passion than anyone else. If anything, they are more susceptible. They are exposed to every kind of emotional and spiritual sickness. Only those who are spiritually empty seek their help. Like medical doctors who are daily exposed to deadly germs of disease, if they are not constantly on guard, constantly inoculated, under constant control of the Holy Spirit, they fall. Satan always seems to aim his biggest guns at the man on the point in spiritual warfare. Thus it should never come as a shock that shepherds are usually the first ones to bleed when the wolf comes after the sheep.

After a great deal of weeping and praying (mostly over the shame of being caught; for true repentance does not come easily, nor rapidly), my friend finally confessed to his wife, to his children and to a few select leaders in the church. There was a genuine attempt on the part of the men to work things out, to keep it quiet and bring healing to their shepherd. But the rumor spread rapidly. In a horrible moment of disclosure, he stood in the pulpit one Sunday morning and confessed to the entire congregation.

The desire to fight, the desire to minister ever again had been squeezed from him by the public recognition of his own imperfection. In shame and confusion, he fled the city. He and his family still smelled of the fires of hell when he arrived at our little city of refuge in Florida.

Healing—no more than repentance—does not come quickly in such situations. What at first may seem to be only a moral slip or an indiscretion is usually nothing less than the emerging tip of an iceberg of spiritual emptiness. The more you examine the thing, the bigger it is. Woe to the man who attempts to minister in such a situation unless he is thoroughly committed to the risk involved, and thoroughly controlled by the Holy Spirit in all his actions. The fool forgives and forgets. The wise man forgives and remembers and stands beside the wounded one with support and direction as the Holy Spirit administers His chastening whip and His purging fire.

Since Jackie and I had opened our lives—and our home—to the healing of wounded warriors, shepherds and sheep alike, there was no way we could back down from this challenge. Fortunately God had provided, in the elders of the Tabernacle Church, a community of love and trust, an atmosphere not based on judgments but on the anticipation of healing. All nine of the elders had emerged, to some degree or another, from similar fires. Jackie and I were with my friend—and his wife—almost daily. On Sundays they sat in the back of the auditorium, hidden in the crowd. Although he had preached for me on several occasions across the years, and many in the congregation knew of his famous work in the other city, we never recognized his presence. Nor did he want me to identify him, so intense was his shame, so deep his sense of failure, so depressed his mood. However, because we recognized him as a man of God, a spiritual leader, albeit a fallen leader, the elders confirmed he should join us in our all-day weekly meetings. Just to sit. And listen. And by being exposed to spiritual health, be encouraged and medicated toward healing.

Some of my friends, hearing he was in Melbourne, called and said, "Don't touch him. He'll drag you down with him." But that is one of the risks a man runs when he reaches out to help. It is the risk a lifeguard has to face when he goes after a drowning man, that he, too, may be pulled beneath the waters—used as a vain stepping stone for another's carnal salvation. Fortunately, I wasn't out there alone. The other ministers in our church were standing with me—counseling, loving, accepting, correcting. It was a perfect example of the Body of Christ reaching out to an injured member, surrounding him with love in an attempt to support and care while the Holy Spirit brought healing.

Any man who commits adultery also lies. Like alcoholism, the two sins always exist side by side. The very nature of any sin which grows in darkness calls for lies to support it. Yet there is no way for a man of God to lie to his Creator, any more than Adam could keep his sin from the Father. Still there remains that eternal desire to hang on to the dregs of sin, to turn loose only as much as you are forced to release—always holding to the vain hope that sometime, somewhere, you can return to the garden where you violated God's command and once again taste of the forbidden fruit. The mere fact that the door is forever closed, that there now stands an angel with a flaming sword prepared to burn the life out of any who attempt to return, is a truth too large to comprehend, too heavy to bear. So healing—and forgiveness—must be administered bit by bit, with love and yet with sternness by men who, themselves, have conceded to the demands of God and have no desire to go in any direction except that directed by the Holy Spirit.

So I struggled with my friend, knowing at times he was lying to me, yet understanding. For to make full disclosure of all the darkness in his heart would expose him to the full light of healing—a light which he was not yet prepared to receive. Thus Jackie and I found ourselves, on the eve of my intention to pull aside and finish the writing of this book, deeply enmeshed in the twisted relationships of a man with his wife, with his mistress (and her husband) and with God. It was exhausting, yet we sensed always that if he could be plucked as a brand from the burning, he would emerge as a giant in the Kingdom—for black sheep always make the most understanding shepherds.

Gradually we began seeing evidence of his restoration. I knew my friend would not only be totally restored by the loving Body of Christ in Melbourne and through the grace of God, but I knew he would eventually take his place in pastoral leadership among our elders (something which has indeed taken place just recently). However, until that happened, I knew we were in for intense, fierce battles as he and his wife fought their way to the surface of their deception where they could breathe the fresh air of truth spoken in love. But even as this was developing, a second minister friend burst on the scene with a similar situation.

It was early one Wednesday morning when he called. I had met him a number of months before when I was speaking at a conference in one of the Gulf states. He had come to me after

26

the service, following a message in which I had alluded to God's forgiveness as experienced in my own life. We sat in the back of the darkened church auditorium while he confided in me. He was in deep trouble. Rebelling against a strained relationship with his wife, he had turned to a woman half his age—a single girl who was the daughter of a prominent family in the city. Now she was pregnant. He had confessed to his wife and resigned his ministerial charge. He knew, if he was ever to serve the Lord again, he would have to do it through reconciliation with his wife—despite this horrible mistake. We sat and talked for a long time. I finally told him to go to another pastor in town, confess to him and seek his guidance. I had returned to Melbourne and forgotten about the whole matter.

Then, Wednesday morning. I had been out of town the day before and had not gotten to bed until long after midnight. I was still asleep when the phone rang at 8 A.M. He was in town. He needed to talk to me.

I agreed to meet him in a private place, and we sat and talked. Although he had been reconciled with his wife, he knew he could no longer remain in the same town with the pregnant girl. The entire community was aware of the situation. The girl had decided to keep her baby; her parents were going to help her raise it. Even though he and his wife had agreed he should pay all the medical expenses for his child, he realized neither of them could stand the stress of remaining in the same community. Their only leading was to move to Melbourne. Would we accept them?

We talked for hours. It was time to speak tough love. If he came, he would have to find a job. He would have to submit to spiritual authority. I suspected this was not just a single experience in his life. Like the others, when we got to know him better, we would find the brown spot on the peeling was the result of a rotten core. He nodded and wept.

But I was asking too much. I watched him, sadly, as he got in his van and left town. I knew he would not be back.

When I returned to the house Jackie was waiting, sitting at the breakfast room table. "Are you ready for another one?" she asked.

27

"Who now?" I said.

"Bill Patillo*," she replied. "He called from the airport. Someone has gone to pick him up."

I slumped into a chair and said, "You better get ready. There are some things about Bill I haven't told you."

A dynamic preacher with Italian ancestry, Bill had been an evangelist before taking a small church and building it to a large congregation. The first time he and his wife visited us in Florida he was near an emotional collapse. Like the others, he was emotionally involved with several women in the congregation. It was tearing him apart, for he recognized his life style was in diametric opposition to the teachings of the Bible concerning marital fidelity

I had listened, counseled briefly, and then kept my mouth shut. I had seen him on several occasions since, but his situation had been worsening. No one else knew, but he was fearful his secret would eventually leak out. Now it seemed I should at least share this with Jackie before Bill arrived.

The rest of the afternoon was spent in intense counsel with this great preacher whose life was a torturous sham. Like the others, he was determined to either break from the demonic bondage which clutched at his viscera or break from the ministry. Long into the evening we talked, wept and prayed. The next day he spent most of the time with a fellow minister in our church who has a ministry of deliverance. That night we were together again. He was rejoicing over what seemed to be a new freedom but still fearful of what he would face when he returned to his church. When I put Bill on the plane early the next morning, he said, "I may have to resign my church and leave the city." Then he asked, "If I come here and get a job, will you receive me?"

That night Jackie and I lay awake for long hours. I needed to talk. "Why me, Lord?" This intense time with my wounded friends had uncovered areas of spiritual scar tissue in my own life which, although healed, were still capable of being inflamed. "Why bring me these fallen shepherds?"

Jackie let me talk, long into the night, for she knew I was hurting. Not for myself but for my friends. Lying on my back beside her, hands clasped under my head, I stared up into the darkness of

* Bill's name has been changed. The facts are true.

our bedroom. "Surely there is some way a man can come to whole-ness without having to be exposed to the purging fire of hell."

"All fire is not from hell," Jackie said softly. "Remember our God is a consuming fire. Sometimes it is He who purges His child-ren. Have you forgotten?"

I had not forgotten. I would never forget. I recalled my own fiery pits, when the flames were so hot I thought surely I would be consumed. I wished that on no man, especially such great and talented men of God as I had been with the previous few days. Yet how else could they be separated from that which was slowly strangling them—knowing if they did not release it they would surely die?

"Is there not some other way for the Holy Spirit to take control of a person's life without forcing him through such agony?" I moaned out loud, feeling the tears gathering in my eyes.

"All people are not the same," Jackie said, her voice still sooth-ingly soft. "Some grow up good. Think of Corrie ten Boom. She accepted the Lord at the age of five and never turned from Him—not a day of her life."

"But even she had to go through the horror of a Nazi concentra-tion camp," I countered.

"True," Jackie answered. "But her struggles were external—with forces from the outside. Not with internal forces like you—and your friends who are being drawn to you like magnets—have to face. You have to fight your battles on a different level. Yet the final conclusion is always the same—God brings you to that place in life where you have no choice but to turn loose."

I remembered the passage of scripture I had quoted to one of the men the day before:

See that ye refuse not him that speaketh: for if they escaped not who refused him that spake on earth, much more shall not we escape, if we turn away from him that speaketh from heaven . . . And this word, yet once more, signifieth the removing of those things that are shaken, as of things that are made, that those things which cannot be shaken may remain. Wherefore we receiving a kingdom which cannot be moved, let us have grace, whereby we may serve God acceptably with reverence and godly fear: For our God is a consuming fire (Hebrews 12:25, 27–29).

God, it seems, judges His ministers by a higher standard. That means He chastens those whom He loves and shakes those for whom He has special purpose, until all the loose things are shaken out and only the firm structure remains—a structure upon which the Holy Spirit can hang the flesh of Jesus Christ. It is a special purpose realized only beyond the control of individual design and desire.

"There was a time," Jackie said gently, reaching over and touching my shoulder in the darkness, "when you thought your world had come to an end. Remember?"

This time the tears overflowed. I remembered. Yet that day was the finest day in my life. For it was that day I turned loose. I relinquished control. I look back to that day of relinquishment, that day when in total and utter desperation I said to God, "Take me. I am worthless." It was the day when the Holy Spirit began to move in greatest power. Perhaps there is no other way. Even so, the knowledge that God is always in control, always standing and waiting for us to get beyond our own control so He can direct our footsteps, is all the hope one really needs. If He could set my feet upon a solid rock and give me a new song, then He could do it with my friends also.

The events, the sensations, the feelings of my own pain are forever etched on my mind. How foolish I had been those long years before. Fresh out of seminary. Flushed with the knowledge I was a success in the ministerial profession. Pastor of one of the largest churches in the state. Yet it had all fallen around me. As I thought back, I knew what had taken place was inevitable, for something always moves into a vacuum. There was no one else to blame. I could have blamed my seminary professors for not teaching me about the baptism in the Holy Spirit. But what guarantee is a charismatic experience to galvanize against sin? Was another baptism necessary—a baptism of fire? The gnawing for love which was deep inside of me had been almost cannibalistic—seeking to devour any around me who seemed willing to be consumed. All ministers (indeed, most ministers) do not turn to other women. Some fill the vacuum with their work. They build great cathedrals, they are nominated to important positions, they are recognized by the media or they lose themselves in legitimate ministry to the poor, the underprivileged, to those in foreign lands. They may join a community or submit themselves to some disciple-maker. Yet even these, eventually, have to examine themselves and face the fact they are created empty. No horizontal relationship will ever satisfy that vertical longing. And no experience—not a salvation experience, not even the baptism of the Holy Spirit—will satisfy that hunger. It can come only when one is *filled* with—and controlled by—the Holy Spirit.

And that is not an experience—it is a daily process.

The psychology of why I turned aside will have to be left to another book—and another time. The point I must make here is that because of a prior commitment to God through Jesus Christ, when I did fall I was not utterly cast down.

I trace that commitment and my subsequent spiritual journey back to a time when I was 21 years old. My father and mother, having come into a new and dynamic relationship with God, had insisted their number three son accompany them on a spiritual retreat sponsored by evangelist Jack Wyrtzen at his Word of Life Camp at Schroon Lake, New York. That week, during the summer between my junior and senior years of college, I had made a willful decision to commit my life to Jesus Christ. It was not a dramatic thing. I did not do anything. I did not answer an invitation, walk an aisle or even raise my hand. Rather, alone on a hillside on an island in the lake, I looked up at the stars and said quietly in my spirit, "Jesus Christ, I give you my life. You are my Lord."

At that time several spiritual principles went to work in my life. One of them is covered in some detail in *Risky Living*. When a man commits his life to Jesus Christ as Lord, he voluntarily surrenders the right to choose or the power to vary the consequences of that decision. He is called to move beyond his own control. In other words, from that time on, God can do whatever He wants

31

with that life to bring it to the place it conforms to the image of His Son, Jesus Christ. That is what the Lordship of Jesus Christ is all about. Whatever forces God chooses to bring to bear on that life, external forces like the Nazi concentration camp in Tante Corrie's life or internal forces like the raging sexual and emotional drives confessed by my friends—all are designed and directed by God to bring us to a place of total submission to His Holy Spirit. If that sounds like God allows a person to fall into adultery or allows him to kill someone and wind up in prison so he can hear the Gospel and be saved, then interpret it as you will. Perhaps that is what Augustine called the *felix culpa*—which loosely translated means the "happy sin." I do not have the final answers on whether God causes a thing to happen or allows it to happen. But I do know that once a decision is made to commit a life to Jesus Christ, whether it is in a foxhole, in a jail cell, in a Sunday school department or on the side of a hill on an island in a northern lake—God takes that commitment seriously. If a man drifts, or tries to run away, or even attempts to break the contract—it is indissoluble as far as God is concerned.

The other spiritual principle which I believe went to work in my life back in 1953 is found in that passage on the eternal nature of vows in Deuteronomy 23. Here Moses is giving the children of Israel a new look at the unchanging nature of God.

> When thou shalt vow a vow unto the Lord thy God, thou shalt not slack to pay it: for the Lord thy God will surely require it of thee; and it would be sin in thee . . . That which is gone out of thy lips thou shalt keep and perform . . (Deuteronomy 23:21, 23).

Therefore, even though there was a long period of time—12 years to be exact—between the time I made the vow and the time God required it of me, the spiritual principle was never invalidated. God was just waiting for the right time in my life, waiting until I had run my ego course, waiting as He did with my own parents, until I had to face the fact I could not make it on my own; waiting as He does with alcoholics who all have to come to

32

that point of admitting that life has become "unmanageable" and must be turned over to a higher power, before He chose to step in and require that vow which had gone out of my lips.

As with Moses, who was discovered after having killed the Egyptian and driven into the desert, so I was discovered. I knew it would happen, eventually. There is no way that sin will not eventually come to the surface, especially when it involves a man of God. If Moses could not escape the exposure of his sin, if David could not escape his adulterous relationship with Bathsheba and had to stand exposed before history, why should I expect special favors? That which God seems to tolerate in some, He will not tolerate in those He has thrust into leadership. Thus exposure comes, not for the sake of punishment, but for the sake of salvation. Fortunate is the man who is exposed early in life. Pity the man who is smart enough to hide his sin until the judgment.

Etched forever in my memory are the events that took place the night of exposure. Like Jacob at Peniel, I wrestled—and lost. October 1965. I sat in the beautiful conference room of that large Baptist church in South Carolina, surrounded by a group of 20 deacons, all with stern faces. They had tried over the last few months to convince me to resign. They knew something was wrong but until this dreadful night had found no evidence. As the months of suspicion continued, I hung on. To leave would mean admission of guilt. Worse, it would mean leaving behind a relationship in which I reveled with the same degree of intensity an alcoholic does with his bottle.

Twice before I had stood before the church at the monthly business meeting and gone through a "vote of confidence." Twice I had bluffed my way through. But this time there was concrete evidence. One of the deacons had discovered a note. I had been laid bare. My insides were churning. Desperately I tried to hold the façade of false confidence.

They asked me to leave the meeting and wait outside as they discussed the matter. Instead of at least a pretense at a sedate exit, I bolted. Fled. I stumbled into the darkened sanctuary and knelt at the front, weeping in fear and confusion. Back in the conference room the men were deciding my fate. In the next room

33

was a small office. I called Jackie. "Come get me. I can't take it anymore." I hung up and in a state of near shock, shame and faced with the awfulness of it all, I wandered down a flight of stairs lit dimly by only the quiet redness of an exit light.

She found me, the shepherd of the flock, crouched in a fetal position in a basement hallway, huddled against the landing of the stairs. "It would be better for you, for the children, for this church if I were dead," I sobbed.

She comforted. She soothed. She never asked for details. There was no need. She led me by the hand through the dark hallways of the house of God to our car parked under the lighted window of the conference room. I did not realize it at the time, but those men were God's servants—sent by the Holy Spirit to perform the unpleasant task of shaking a man of God until only the unshakable remained.

That night I walked into the front yard of our beautiful parsonage. Standing under the autumn sky, I looked up into the heavens and screamed: "Take me! Take me now! Quickly!" In a desperate move, I grabbed my shirt and ripped it open at the chest, tearing the buttons and hem as I exposed my bare chest to the heavens, waiting for the inevitable flash of lightning which I knew would come and split me asunder, carrying me into the hell where I belonged.

But there was no flash of lightning, for the purging fire had already begun to burn. And besides, God does not punish sin the way we punish it. As ranchers often burn off a pasture to kill the weeds so the new grass can sprout, so the consuming fire of God burns away the dross without consuming the sinner.

There was more to follow, of course. For one thing, we had to leave. Then there was the fear of going to sleep at night because I could not stand the thought of waking to a new day. Better to sit up sleepless nights than sleep and start a new day without trumpets in the morning. There was the desperate reaching out for friends, only to find they had all deserted. I was like a leper. Unclean. I wrote letters—more than 90 of them—to pastoral and denominational friends. Only one man dared respond and that was with a curt, "I received your letter and shall be praying for you."

Perhaps God was working here too; comfort or encouragement

34

at that agonizing time could have moved me even deeper into a continuing self-deceiving sense of feeling justified.

And anyway, what else could anyone say?

We returned to my home state of Florida, to a small but rapidly growing church—the only opportunity that was open. But as Vance Havner once remarked, it doesn't do any good to change labels on an empty bottle. Nothing inside me had changed. I was still the magnificent manipulator, the master of control, the defender of my position. I was still pushing people around. I was far more politician than a man of God. The Holy Spirit was not controlling my life

Soon echoes from the past began drifting down to Florida—rumors of adultery, of manipulation, of lying. The old undertow of fear sucked at my guts. I was about to be swept back to sea for I had not been honest with the committee which had interviewed me for the Florida position. I could feel the insidious inevitability of confrontation creeping upon me again. I continued to fight, to brave the growing onslaught of fact that kept building the case against me. It took 15 months of a stormy relationship before the Florida church cast me into the waves to calm the sea—just like Jonah

The crisis exploded one Sunday morning when I stepped up to the pulpit to preach On the pulpit stand was a petition asking me to resign. It was signed by 350 people, many of whom were sitting, smiling in the congregation. A group of men had hired a private detective and checked into my past. The detective's report—all 47 pages of badly distorted facts—had been duplicated and handed out to the congregation. The deacons demanded I take a lie detector test. Even though I passed it—declaring I had no intention of perpetrating upon that new church the sins of my past—it was not enough. I had no choice but once again to slink home and huddle with my wife and children while the fire of God continued its purging work.

Often, I have discovered, we cannot hear God when we are busy. Hearing comes only when we have taken—or are forced to take—times of quietness. With Moses it took 40 years of wandering in the burning sands of the Sinai, tending the sheep and goats of

35

Jethro, his father-in-law and the priest of Midian, on the backside of the desert. It took that long for the fire of God to purge him of all the pride of his Egyptian prestige. Only then was he able to hear. Only then, when everything was quiet, did the angel of the Lord appear in the flame of fire out of the midst of the bush which burned but was not consumed. When a man has many things to do, he often does not have time to turn aside and see great sights. His time is consumed with busyness, his mind with activity. But Moses had time. So when the bush burned on the side of Mt. Horeb, he left his grazing flock and climbed the side of the rocky mountain to investigate. Then it was that God spoke to him and gave him direction.

So it was with me. All activity had ceased. No longer did I have to attend important committee meetings. No longer did I have to supervise budgets, direct visitation programs, promote an attendance campaign or even prepare sermons. All that I had felt was important was taken from me. There was nothing to do but tend the few sheep and goats who had pulled out of the church with me and were huddled together on the hillside grazing. I was beyond my own control. Then my bush burned.

Someone, perhaps my mother, had entered a subscription in my name for *Guideposts* magazine. I seldom read *Guideposts*, but in my idle time, which I now had in great abundance, I picked it up. Someplace in that particular issue I found a half-page announcement of a writers' workshop to be sponsored by the magazine. The stipulations were simple. Submit a first-person manuscript of 1,500 words following the basic *Guideposts'* style. This would be evaluated and judged by an editorial committee who would then pick the best 20 manuscripts. Those selected would receive an all-expense-paid trip to New York and would attend a one-week writers' workshop, conducted by the magazine editors, at the Wainwright House at Rye, New York, on Long Island Sound.

Several years before I had befriended a young man who was preparing to go to South America as a missionary pilot with a group known as the Jungle Aviation and Radio Service, the flying arm of the Wycliffe Bible Translators. I had been intrigued with

Tom Smoak's story. As an Air Force pilot, his jet bomber had exploded in midair over Little Rock, Arkansas. He alone had escaped the burning inferno, falling to the ground with a flaming parachute and barely escaping death as his parachute snagged on the tops of two trees in the backyard of a Christian woman. A friend of Tom's had jotted down the facts and sent them to me. Then along came the *Guideposts* offer. Since I had nothing else to do, I wrote the story and sent it in.

My bush burned on October 1, 1967. I was stretched out on the bed in the back room of our little rented house when the phone rang. It was the Western Union telegraph office. Jackie took the call and copied the message on a scrap of paper. It was from Leonard LeSourd, editor of *Guideposts,* stating I was one of the 20 winners—out of more than 2,000 submissions.

I didn't realize it at the time, but my life was about to take a tremendous turn. There were no outward indications. All I knew was for months I had been floating with the tide, buffeted by whatever circumstances God sent along. I had no sensation of direction, no indication this telegram was anything other than another event which had cropped up in the river. I could either dodge it or confront it. I chose confrontation and sent a return wire stating I accepted their offer and would attend the workshop the following month. Only as I look back on that event—now years in the past— do I realize I should have taken off my shoes. I was on holy ground.

The rest is recorded history and has, to some degree, been covered in my book, *Risky Living.* At the workshop John and Elizabeth Sherrill, both editors for *Guideposts* at the time, were approached by Dan Malachuk, a book publisher who was looking for a writer to compose the story of Nicky Cruz. Nicky was a former Puerto Rican gang leader from New York, now a Pentecostal preacher, whose conversion had played a major part in *The Cross and the Switchblade,* the book John and Elizabeth had written with David Wilkerson. The Sherrills were not interested in the project but recommended me. Before the week was out I had signed an agreement with the publisher and was on my way back to Egypt with a new sense of direction. I was going to become a writer.

Four months later I had an encounter with the Holy Spirit whom, up until that time, I only recognized as a boring phrase in the Doxology. Almost everything about me was revolutionized—instantly. All that has happened since is material for other volumes. The important point I want to make is, I had nothing to do with it. Everything within me had been striving against God. Like Jacob at Peniel, I had been vainly wrestling with the angel of the Lord, trying to have my own way, yet at the same time unwilling to turn loose until he blessed me. Now the blessing had come. And with it, a limp. Yet even the limp—and the scars—are badges of His glory.

Perfection still eludes me. I am still vulnerable. But most important, I am no longer satisfied with my imperfection. Nor, thank God, am I intimidated by it. I have reached the point of recognizing that God uses imperfect, immoral, dishonest people. In fact, that's all there are these days. All the holy men seem to have gone off and died. There's no one left but us sinners to carry on the ministry.

If I had my way I would never again do anything wrong. Yet, like Paul:

For I know that in me (that is, in my flesh,) dwelleth no good thing: for to will is present with me; but how to perform that which is good I find not (Romans 7:18).

Dissatisfied with imperfection, I am now determined to move toward that goal of "conforming to Christ"—knowing at the same time it will never come because of my obedience—but out of my submission to the Holy Spirit. It is that obedience that leads to the fine art of living beyond control—beyond self-will and into the comfort of the Spirit's control.

If I can convey this message to the three friends I mentioned earlier or to anyone else who feels there is no hope, then this book will not be in vain. Yet, at the same time, as I look back over my own life, I wonder if any truth becomes valid or personal until it is burned into our souls by the branding iron of God. I admit I do not know.

Malachi draws the picture of God sitting in front of the melting crucible under which burns the refiner's fire. The fire has been stoked to white heat. In the crucible is silver ore, representing, Malachi says, the "sons of Levi"—those chosen for special service in the Kingdom. The fire is burning, purging the dross until only the pure metal is left. Only when the refiner peers into the crucible and sees the reflection of his own face is the heat turned down and the pure metal poured into the forms which bless the world.

My old friend Seabury Oliver says the only way man—any man—ever comes to know God intimately is through trouble. Perhaps he's right. On the other hand, when I realize that most of my problems, perhaps all my problems, have been self-inflicted, I wonder if all this fire has been necessary. I suspect not. I look at others around me, those who have served God without the rebellious spirit which seems to be so much a part of my makeup, and see they seem to have passed through the fire at very low temperature and intensity. Without much pain or suffering they have come to a beautiful, simple, yet valid understanding of the deep truths of God. Others of us must pass through the very Valley of the Shadow of Death before we can say with a certainty, "My head is anointed. My cup runneth over."

Yet it is in these places, where the awful sins of life threaten to consume us, that we learn God can be trusted. Locking our wings in faith, we soar on the thermal of His Holy Spirit, out of control, yet in His will.

III

Finding Your Place

When I was five years old, my father built what I felt was the most wonderful house in all the world. It had 16 huge rooms and was located on 48 acres of rural Florida woodlands and pasture, with a big citrus grove behind it and a free-flowing, sulfur-water well nearby.

The house was all redwood—inside and out. The floors were knotty pine and the huge staircase was birdseye cypress. Everything else was stained redwood, walls and ceilings. To me it was the most beautiful house in the world—and the most liveable.

A huge attic covered the entire house. There were places to hide under the stairwell and behind the furnace. There were secret closets, dark clothes chutes and woodbins in the kitchen and next to the fireplace in the library.

Nearly all my childhood memories relate to that big house and the property surrounding it. It was my place.

Daddy and Mother had five children, and Daddy said if he had to give them baths he wasn't going to break his neck. So he built a raised, six-foot-long bathtub in one of the upstairs bathrooms. It was three feet off the floor with a set of steps on one end and storage drawers underneath.

It was a marvelous house. It was my fortress, my home, my

security. Behind the house were barns for the cows and ponies we raised, a huge haybarn where the tractors which worked in the grove were kept and lots of little sheds and other ideal places to play and hide. During World War II, when milk and butter were rationed, we had plenty for ourselves and our neighbors. Our chickens gave us eggs, our ponies provided pleasure and occasional money through a sale and the orange and grapefruit groves always produced a good crop.

Through my school years, into college and seminary, I knew I could retreat to the big house if I felt the need. It was warm and filled with life and memories. My mother and dad were always there to protect me. Even if they were not there, the house itself seemed to have a protective personality. I could go up the stairs to my old bedroom, sit on the floor with my arms on the windowsill, look out over the pasture and feel like I was home. The house was everything four boys and a baby sister could ever want.

But when the last of the five children moved away, my parents decided it was time to be practical. Daddy had surrendered his life to the Lord at the age of 60. That meant all he had belonged to God—including the big house and the 48 acres. When there was no more practical reason to maintain the redwood home, he gave it—including most of the 48 acres—to the Florida Baptist Convention to be the home for the Baptist Retirement Center. Mother and Daddy then built a much smaller house nearby and released the big house to be used as the headquarters and home for the administrator. A number of smaller cottages, motel type units and a nursing home were later built in the old pasture and among the citrus trees.

I was in graduate school in Texas when the letter came that the house was gone. Even though I approved of what he had done, there was still a great sense of loss, of sadness. I felt as if my roots had been clipped. For the first time in my life there was no place to go back to. It was a true grief experience as I mourned the passing of the old house.

A number of years later, after our own children were well on their way to adulthood, Jackie and I had a unique experience over a Christmas holiday. We were back in Vero Beach to spend Christmas with our parents.

"How would you like to sleep over in the big house?" Daddy asked, with a twinkle in his eye.

"Do you mean it?"

"They have changed administrators at the retirement center," he explained. "The new director hasn't arrived. The big house is empty if you'd like to stay there for a couple of nights."

It was quite an experience being back in the big house. It was bare except for a few mattresses on the floor. Though most of the furniture was gone, it was still the same house. The electricity had been shut off but there was no need for lights—at least not for me. I had, as a child, memorized every inch of the house. I knew which way the doors opened. I remembered that the third step above the landing on the stairway creaked when you stepped on it. (I had discovered, back in high school when I came in late at night, I should step over that step or run the risk of waking my parents who slept in the bedroom at the top of the stairs.) I knew a certain broom closet would smell of Old English furniture polish where I had spilt an entire bottle when I was a boy. That evening I took the children by the hand and led them from room to room, explaining all that had happened there in years gone by. We looked at the marks on the bathroom closet door where Daddy had measured each of us on New Year's Day to check our growth. We climbed the ladder to the attic and peered down the clothes chute.

Yet it wasn't the same. Nostalgic, certainly. But when I went to bed that night I realized something was different. I didn't belong there anymore. My roots no longer extended backwards into the redwood house. They went in some other direction. It was like looking on the body of a loved one. It looked like it used to. It felt like it used to. But it was dead. My mother and dad, my brothers and sister—they were what made that home alive.

That night I lay awake in the darkness, listening, waiting to hear the whispered voices of my mother and dad in the next room, wondering if I would hear my older brothers laughing down the hall, listening for the gentle breathing of my younger brother in the other bed. But they were gone. My parents lived in another house. My brothers and sister had married and lived in other states. I listened for the sound of the sulfur-water well in the yard, but it had long been capped. I listened for the gentle tick-tocking of the old grandfather clock which had hung on the stairway landing, but it had long since been removed to my parents' new house. Maybe I would hear the shower running or smell the orange blossoms. But the water was shut off and the orange trees had long been bulldozed up to make way for the retirement cottages. The house was still there, but the life was gone.

I realized, though, as I realize even more now, that with the passing of that old house something good had happened in my life. For the first time I was able to have a clear look backward. The house had been a barrier in my life. It had been a place of security, a place where I could run when I was afraid. I always knew, even after I married, that if anything ever happened I could retreat to the big house in Vero Beach. There was always a place where I was welcome. A place where I could belong.

The removal of the house gave me a new perspective into the past. For the first time I was able to look backward beyond my parents, all the way to my true dwelling place—the dwelling place of God.

The same thing happened to me several years later when my father died. He was 87 years old and in declining health, yet his mind and spirit remained clear and lucid. When my mother called, that Sunday after church, and said, "Daddy B has just gone to be with the Lord," Jackie and I were there within the hour— driving down to Vero Beach from our home in Melbourne. We drove past the big house but didn't give it a second look, going directly to the smaller house where my folks had lived the last 20 years of their lives together. We went back into the bedroom where Daddy's body was still warm on the bed. But it wasn't his habitation anymore. The life was gone, missing from the body. I realized that afternoon that somehow another door had been opened to me, a door which would enable me to understand spiritual things even deeper. I would no longer depend on him for guidance. Now I would go beyond him to my heavenly Father.

"I do not wish him back," I said to Jackie, fighting back the tears. "But why do I miss him so?"

"You miss him because you have always gone to him for advice and direction," she said. "But like the big house, he is gone now. And you will be a better man because of it."

She was right. He had become my resting place. My security. If there was something I was getting ready to enter, some kind of business proposition, I'd turn to my dad. I would drive down to Vero Beach, sit beside his bed, make the presentation, and then wait. "Well, what do you think about this?" If I had some kind of spiritual revelation, I'd bounce it off of him. When I finished a new book, I always sent him the very first copy. I would wait a few days and then drive down to Vero Beach, sit beside his bed and wait for a response—like a little boy coming home from school with a picture drawn with crayons waiting for his dad's approval.

But because the big house was there in my past, because my dad was in my past, I never could get all the way back to where I belonged. Enjoying the pools along the way, I never would go all the way to the spring—the source.

Bit by bit these things need to be taken away until we become like Jesus with no place to lay our heads. Foxes have holes, birds have nests, but the true man of God has no place to lay his head but on the bosom of the Father. Places—geographical places—are necessary for service. But not for security.

It was good to go to my dad while he was here on earth, to seek his wisdom. Shortly before he died I drove down to his home in Vero Beach and went back into the bedroom where he was resting. His body, at that time, was almost gone. His old friend, P. J. McGriff, the black man who had long worked as one of his picking crew foremen in the groves, had returned in the latter years to give himself to my daddy during the final years of his life—picking him up off the bed and moving him to the wheelchair, then back to the bed, using arms and shoulders made strong by years of picking up heavy boxes of fruit in the orange groves. P. J. had put Daddy on the bed to rest a while, and I sat down beside him to talk.

I had a scheme which seemed foolproof. It involved making a lot of money—most of which I wanted to return to the Lord. Daddy lay on the bed, his eyes closed, listening as I rattled on, explaining my scheme in great detail. He could tell I was excited.

It seemed to be the answer to the prayer I had been praying for years. But when I had finished and asked him, "Well, what do you think?" he cleared his throat, asked for a tissue to wipe his lips, and spoke. He began by asking questions. Pointed questions.

"Has God specifically told you to do this?"

I stammered.

"Has God told you to stop doing other things which have been extremely productive, in order to spend your time with this?"

I could feel my eyes dilating as he struck at the heart of the matter.

Finally he closed his eyes again and said softly, "Son, never move away from the proven things of God for that which is mere speculation."

I left Vero Beach and drove back to Melbourne a shaken man. My dream castles had been shattered by his keen and incisive questions. But I knew he was right. I knew had I followed through on my scheme, I would have become a businessman, a financier, and would have never had time to write another book—much less carry on my ministry.

I was grateful for my dad's wise counsel, but I also knew—deep in my heart—that God was eager for me to reach the place where I did not have to turn to my earthly father but could turn directly to Him. He was bringing me to the place where I could walk directly into the courts of the Living God and say, "Father, what do You think of this?" and then receive His correction when He said, "Son, I have better things for you. This is the way. Walk ye in it."

As meaningful as my dad and mom are to me, more meaningful are the tabernacles of God. Now I have no old homestead. I have my own home instead. Now I have no father; I am a father instead. All the things which were so precious to me are being taken away so I can find my true place in life, my true security, which always lies in a house not made with hands.

Recently I was in Denver, Colorado, for a business convention. While I was there my old friend Harold Bruce, in town for the same convention, asked me to have breakfast with him. I had known Harold for a number of years, and I was impressed with his Christian commitment as a wealthy businessman from Tucson, Arizona.

Early Tuesday morning I met Harold outside the Brown Palace Hotel promptly at 7:30 A.M. We each had a 9 A.M. engagement in separate places, so I didn't want to be late.

Harold greeted me warmly and we went into the rather plush restaurant. The coffee shop was filled, but we found a table—although the dirty dishes had not yet been cleared. This didn't bother me, since I was happy to see Harold and eager to talk over some exciting business items. Harold, however, was agitated that the table was dirty. I noticed him gingerly pushing away the plate in front of him as though he were afraid the remnants of another person's breakfast still on the plate—the yellow residue of what had once been a fried egg and half a piece of toast—might somehow contaminate him. While I was chatting he kept looking around for the busboy, rapping his fingers on the table. Impatiently.

I didn't pay much attention to his agitation since I was engrossed in our conversation. Occasionally he would seem to forget the dirty dishes in front of him and relax. Shortly however he would glance at his watch, scowl at the table, then look anxiously around the room. Where was that waitress?

"Relax, Harold," I joshed. "They seem to be shorthanded this morning and with the convention in town . . ."

He smiled at me nervously, looked back at his watch, and said, "I guess it doesn't matter if we don't get breakfast, does it?"

"It won't bother me," I said. "The only reason I was going to eat anyway was to be with you. I'm satisfied just to sit here and talk."

But Harold was not satisfied. He kept drumming on the table with his fingertips and glancing around the room. Finally he interrupted me in the middle of a sentence. "There's no sense in waiting around like this. I'm going to find a waitress." And he was gone.

He had no sooner disappeared than a waitress appeared—with the busboy. While he cleared the table and replaced the tablecloth, she apologized. They had a capacity crowd and two of the waitresses were sick. She was handling the entire dining room by herself.

I ordered, looked around for Harold, and apologized back to her.

47

"I don't know where my friend is," I said.

"Oh, I know where he is," she said, nodding toward the cash register. "He's over there complaining." Moments later Harold returned. The waitress reappeared, took his order and left. After she had gone I told him what she had said.

"Do you know what the waitress said about you while you were gone?"

He blanched and just looked at me.

I continued. "I apologized because you were gone and said I didn't know where you were. She said she knew where you were. You were over there complaining."

Very slowly he pulled off his glasses and looked at me. Then tears came to his eyes. "I don't know why I can't hold still. I don't know why I'm so restless. I feel insecure—as if I can't settle down in *my* place and feel comfortable—secure." The rest of the morning was spent discussing real security—that which one can find only in Christ.

The Swiss psychiatrist, Paul Tournier, said: "Every man needs a place to be." A place where we're secure. A place where we belong. A place that is comfortable to us. Every person needs a place of some kind.

In Psalm 84, David captures the heart cry of all men when he writes:

How amiable are thy tabernacles, O Lord of hosts! My soul longeth, yea, even fainteth, for the courts of the Lord: my heart and my flesh crieth out for the Living God.

The New English Bible translates it like this:

How dear is thy dwelling place, thou Lord of Hosts! I pine, I faint with longing for the courts of the Lord's temple.

My favorite translation is in The Amplified Bible:

My soul yearns, yes, even pines and is homesick for the courts of the Lord; my heart and my flesh cry out and sing for joy to the living God.

After Adam's sin, man became a wanderer, a gypsy, a pilgrim. His place in perfect fellowship with God was shattered. His home in the garden denied. A great angel was put at the door to deny him entrance. Ever since then man has been a wanderer—striving to discover who he is and where he belongs.

No baby is born peaceful. Babies are born grasping, looking for a place. We grow up restless. We can't stay still. We have to jump up and find the waitress. It is the spirit of the wanderlust.

Not being able to find our place in God, we try to localize Him. We build buildings and call them "houses of God." Unable to have a personal relationship, we insist on formalized prayer, bowing our heads, closing our eyes, going into the chapel, dropping on our knees—trying to nail God down for a few minutes so we can have a temporary place.

The Episcopal priest, Malcolm Boyd, worked his way through the rigid requirements of the church to ordination. Then, unfulfilled, he became involved in social activism. Later he dropped out of any kind of Christ-centered ministry and finally wrote a lurid book describing his homosexual way of life. Always looking. Never finding. But anger is not the right emotion to express toward the Malcolm Boyds. It should be pity. For there is something of them in every one of us. It's what I was looking for in those early years of my ministry. It's what my three friends in the last chapter were looking for. It is the story of Everyman—always looking for his place.

Jesus, in a magnificent briefing with His disciples, told them He had a job for them. "I send you out as sheep in the midst of wolves," He said in Matthew 10:16. But as we read on, we find Jesus gave them absolutely no instructions on how to contact Him in case of an emergency. What discipler would send his disciples out without giving them the hot-line number back to the church? But Jesus had a purpose in this. He was training them for the time which was to come when He would be gone and they would have to depend entirely on an invisible Spirit to lead them. Now He was there in the flesh. But the time was soon to come when He would no longer be among them. No longer visible. He wanted each man to have an independent relationship with God Himself.

That was the whole purpose of Jesus' ministry among men—to bring men to a place of independent relationship with God. He did not want them related to an earthly disciple-maker the rest of their lives. He knew His followers would have to function everywhere. Alone in courtrooms. In jails. In the quiet of their homes. In the jungles, when nobody else was within a hundred miles. They needed to learn to stand alone, if necessary, simply having fellowship with the invisible Spirit.

When you go out with Jesus, you burn all the bridges, you relinquish the past, you willingly venture toward a new place. Only then can the Holy Spirit have complete control.

The Bible pictures life as a pilgrimage. We are here for a season, then we move on. All incidents on earth are but training sessions for that which comes later. If we stop at any given place—at a house, at a relationship, even at an experience (no matter how wonderful it is), then we miss what God has for us down the line.

Let our hearts be homesick for the courts of God—not for what lies in the past. If there is to be nostalgia, let it be for what is yet to come, not for what was.

The night before He died, Jesus called His disciples together in an upper room and said, "In my Father's house are many mansions: if it were not so, I would have told you. I go to prepare a place for you. And if I go and prepare a place for you, I will come again, and receive you unto myself; that where I am, there ye may be also" (John 14:2, 3).

Notice. Jesus is not the place. He is the One who prepares the place. Neither is Jesus our refuge. In Psalm 46 David says, "The eternal God is our refuge." Who then is Jesus? Jesus is the Son of the eternal God. Jesus is not the place. Jesus is the way. No man comes to the place but by Him. What then is the place? The place is the courts of the Lord. "My soul yearns, yes, even pines and is homesick for the courts of the Lord; my heart and my flesh cry out and sing for joy to the living God."

We seldom talk about the Father anymore. We do a lot of talking about Jesus—and in some circles even more talking about the Holy Spirit. That is wonderful. But the purpose of Jesus' mission on earth was to reconcile men to the Father—to make the rough places plain, the crooked places straight—so we could enter into the courts of the Father with Him. When the child of God understands that he is as welcome in the presence of the Father as the incarnate Son of God is welcome, then he has an entirely new concept of who he is. It is magnificent. Much more magnificent than most of us can grasp. The eternal God is my refuge, my dwelling place, my place of security—where soaring is a venture in safety.

God allows His children certain crutches to lean upon—spiritual training wheels, so to speak. We find them all the way through history, for God knows we are a weak people. The Ark of the Covenant was a crutch. The Temple in Jerusalem was a crutch. But God was constantly weaning His people away from the crutches to teach them to stand alone in their place. God is not contained in buildings. He is spirit. He is your place.

I was with a Roman Catholic priest in Bangkok last year. He was working in the most miserable situation I had ever seen, in the slums of Bangkok. He lived in a slaughterhouse, sleeping in a tiny corner and spending his time with the people. The smell was abominable. The conditions too ghastly to describe. He took me around, showing me where he worked, introducing me to his Thai friends.

I finally stopped him. "Father, where are you from?"

He looked at me in amazement. "I'm from Bangkok."

"No," I said, "I mean, where is your home?"

"Oh," he said, "Bangkok is my home."

I finally had to pin him down with good plain American lingo. "I mean, where were you born?"

"Oh, now I understand," he said with a grin. "I was born in Portland, Oregon. I went to college in Oregon and seminary in Chicago. But I'm from Bangkok. This is my place."

No wonder he could sleep in that stinking slaughterhouse. He had found his place—not in Bangkok, but in God.

It's difficult to understand that—for God is invisible and we are looking for something tangible. A roof over our heads, someone to hold our hand, a lap to sit on. That's the reason we want to return to the old homestead, or visit the cemetery and place flowers every Saturday morning on our mother's grave, or carry the torch for some old flame vowing we'll never marry. That's the reason many widows refuse to consider a second marriage; their dead husbands remain their "place"—rather than the living God. But the call of God is to move upward: beyond mother and daddy, beyond that aunt or uncle who was so meaningful to us, beyond that grayhaired grandmother who let us sit on her lap or snuggle into bed beside her, beyond that old house where we were raised as a child, beyond the childhood romance and all the misspent dreams of how it could have been, beyond all that to the tabernacles of God. In the abiding place of God there is satisfaction for every need. "My soul is homesick for the courts of the Lord."

Heaven is not precious to me because my dad is there. That is a precious hope, but that is not the thing that draws me to Heaven. The great drawing toward Heaven is because it is the final court of God, the ultimate in entering into His tabernacle. It is the abiding place of Him who has loved me, sustained me, carried me through, given me dreams and hopes, filled my life with happy memories, led me through the rough places and given me light in the darkness. That's who I long for.

The writer of Hebrews says we are strangers in exile. We are wanderers, travelers. We are like Abraham who was called of God to leave his "place" in Ur and go out, not knowing where he was going. He became a wanderer. Why? Because God wanted a man whose place was in a relationship—not in a location. We are all cast in the design of Abraham, modern day Hebrews, nomads living in temporary lodgings. Earth is not our home; we are just passing through.

In Hebrews, Paul had already warned that little community of Christians that they faced two dangers. He said the first danger was drifting away from the faith. The second danger was failing to mature in the faith. Then he warned them of the greatest peril of all—losing your sense of direction in the faith. He constantly had to remind his readers they were citizens of two worlds. They were not bound by traditions nor obligated to those who had gone on before: they were moving on toward a tabernacle whose builder

52

and maker is God. Again we are being asked to move beyond our own control—to venture into a Spirit-controlled relationship with God.

The quest of man for his place—and his penchant for localizing it with something concrete—is perhaps the biggest spiritual problem mankind faces.

In *Fiddler on the Roof,* Tevye says that the thing which is most important in life is "Tradition!" That's the reason, he says, the Jews have been able to live through all their persecutions and keep their identity. Yet, as necessary as tradition is, it is also the thing which keeps us from moving on. For man is constantly in danger of stopping to dig a well, build an altar, and settle into some kind of overnight tradition—much like those groups who brashly announce "first annual meetings."

Men in business and industry vie for place. Security for many comes by having a "V.P." after their name, their name on a parking sign in the executive lot, or their own washroom connecting to their office. All these are more than status symbols—they are symbols of having "arrived"—of having a place.

So we put crosses on our lapels, or dove tags on our cars, to signify our arrival at "place."

(I have a friend who had a dove tatooed on his chest. He says, "When they take me into the funeral home, they will know I'm charismatic.")

There is nothing wrong with dove tags, lapel crosses or having our name on the sign—as long as it does not become traditionalized and become our "place" of security. The first thing King Hezekiah did when he took office in the nation of Israel was to destroy the bronze serpent which had been passed down from generation to generation. It was the same bronze serpent Moses had lifted up in the wilderness to protect the people from the snakes. It had been preserved as part of the tradition, passed down through the generations as a good luck charm. But by the time Hezekiah took office the people were actually worshiping it. It had become their place. So he had it destroyed, for he wanted the people to find their place in God.

It is all part of mankind's problem in trying to localize God.

For almost nine years I was the pastor of a very traditional Baptist church in South Carolina. When I took over as senior minister, however, following a building program, the finance committee was deeply worried about paying for the new pews. They were beautiful pews—28 rows of them—mahogany colored with white ends. We had long pews in the middle—20-seaters—and short pews on the sides—five-seaters. But they weren't paid for and the bill was past due.

At an emergency meeting of the finance committee, someone had a good idea. "Let's put bronze plaques on the ends of the pews," one of the men suggested. "We can put the people's names on them. We'll sell the pews—$250 for the long ones and $150 for the short ones."

The church had tried for a year to raise the money unsuccessfully. But when they agreed to put the names of people on them, they raised the money in four days. And there were another 30 families who offered to give money, but it was too late.

God allows us crutches. Putting bronze plaques on pews is a crutch. It takes time to recognize we serve a God who is capable of healing cripples.

Once the pews in our church were paid for, we noticed a strange thing beginning to take place. The people who had their names on the pews began to sit in them—as though they actually belonged to them. No one said anything about it, but several of us noticed it. However, since all the rest of us in the church—including myself—were busy establishing our own place, we did nothing more than notice.

As for me, I found my place in more subtle ways. On Sunday mornings the church staff entered the sanctuary in ascending order of importance. First came the organist and pianist who took their seats at the instruments. Then the choir filed in from two special doors in the back of the choir loft and stood before the congregation. Then from the right, front corner arrived the ministerial procession. First came the educational director, next the minister of music, followed by the associate pastor and then me. All of us had our place.

One Sunday morning we went through our little ritual (it was

54

something like firing the cannon at dawn), and I arrived on the platform and stood, as usual, looking out over the congregation. The auditorium was comfortably filled (which, according to Charles Allen, means everyone had room to lie down). But when I glanced to my left, I noticed something strange.

The regular seating place for the professor, his wife, and the three old maid sisters was four rows back in one of the five-seater pews—the one with the professor's name on it, of course. The professor was actually a retired sixth grade school teacher, but like many in the congregation, he was still vying for place. It was natural for him to cling to the title of professor.

That morning, however, not only were the professor and his wife and the three old maid sisters in the pew, but there were two other people squeezed in beside them. And I mean *squeezed*. The five-seater pews were meant for five people—and that's all. Adding two more was next to impossible. But there they were, all crammed in there like vienna sausages in a can. And the odd thing was, there were a number of other seats close by.

When they stood to sing, they all had to stand up at the same time. To sit down meant they had to go down in unison—as if they were welded together.

It wasn't until after the service that one of the ushers told me what had happened. "You won't believe this," he said laughing. "But those two strangers came in early. They didn't know that pew 'belonged' to the professor, and they sat down there. When the professor and his group arrived, instead of splitting up or moving to another pew, they crammed in there with them."

At the time I thought it was ridiculous. Now I understand. The human drive for man to find his place is one of the strongest of all forces.

"I've got my friend. That makes me secure."

"General Motors is my place. That is where I belong."

"I've joined the labor union. The Teamsters will take care of me from now on. They are my place."

It's built into all of us. Little girls want to play house. Little boys have their secret clubs. College students have their sororities and fraternities to which they pledge themselves for ever and ever.

55

The secret handclasp, the password, the fraternal ring: they all signify that we belong.

When I was checking out of the hotel in Denver, the fighting men of the 94th Infantry were checking in. These were the men who had fought under General Patton in World War II. There they were. Fat men crammed into their old Eisenhower jackets complete with shoulder patches, wearing their 30-year-old army hats. That was their place—the memory of the past. Once a year they would get together, calling each other "Sarge" and "Captain" and get so drunk they couldn't remember anything. The 94th Infantry was their place.

With others it's the Volunteer Fire Department, the Masons, the Rotary, the Lions, the Kiwanis or even the church.

"What do you mean, I can't play the piano anymore? That's my place."

"But we've got a much better pianist now, and you hit all the wrong notes. Besides, you get mad and slam the lid down during the sermon if the preacher says something you don't like."

"I don't care. My daddy gave that piano to the church, and I have always played it. That's where I belong, and I'll stay there until hell freezes over."

Maturity is the ability to move from the downstairs concepts of things we can touch, smell and taste—to the upstairs concepts of things spiritual.

I recently read an article on "executive mobility." That's a system top corporation executives use to produce people as singlemindedly devoted to their corporation as they are. The idea is to move the junior executives around so often that the only things left in their lives are money, work and power. If you keep separating a man from his friends, his community, even his family, after a while he will begin to believe the only stable thing in life is his job—and he'll throw himself into his work with total abandon for the sake of rising to the top where he won't have to move anymore. The trouble with that is, he'll either die at an early age—burned out for Amalgamated Fertilizer Corporation—or in his effort to get ahead quickly, he'll make a horrible mistake and be fired.

It happens all the time.

Rare is the business executive who is able to determine his place apart from his next job offer. For that reason, people in America are constantly on the go—moving from city to city, transferred by their job or seeking a new job. A few of these carry their "place" with them. Most of them are still searching.

Recently I visited in the home of an old man who had been in the nursery and greenhouse business all his life. "I'm an author, too," he said seriously.

"Oh, I didn't know."

"Oh, yes," he said, pointing to a yellowed clipping which was framed behind glass and hanging near the fireplace next to an award for growing the finest nasturtiums for the county fair. I walked over to the frame. It was a letter to the editor giving an opinion on why people should not vote for Franklin D. Roosevelt for a third term for president. His name was printed at the bottom.

It was his place.

We see it in church—this desire to belong. "If I can only be elected president of my Sunday school class." "At last, I've been elected as a deacon." Or, "Hey, everybody! I'm the person who washes the communion glasses."

It's not wrong to feel this way. The problems come when that place is not provided, or worse, when it is taken away from us.

How do we find our place?

First, we find it by confessing we are lost and looking. Salvation is a process which starts at an experience and continues for the rest of our earthly lives. There is a sense in which things are settled, finished, at salvation. This is true of our eternal security, for instance. But when it comes to finding our place on earth—to moving into maturity—then salvation is a process which continues until death. It is a never-ending process—this process of being saved.

Second, we find our place by recognizing the basic difference between a citizen and a tourist. A citizen has a sense of permanency, a sense of belonging. If you are a citizen, you buy a home. You settle down. You register and vote. You may even run for public office. You buy a cemetery lot. You put your name on the end of a pew. That is your home.

But citizens of the Kingdom are a different lot. This earth is not their home. They are just passing through. They are pilgrims. They keep their eternal passport in their pockets at all times.

That is the reason God warns His people about being unequally yoked with unbelievers, about being in debt to no man, about staying clear of the world systems which would put us in bondage. God doesn't want us with roots so deep in the earth that when the trumpet sounds, we can't go.

When we moved into the country, my 18-year-old son Tim insisted we buy a pickup truck. "Dad, we can't live out here in the country unless we have a pickup." We started shopping for trucks. Of course the kind Tim wanted had great big oversized tires, roll bars, lights on the top and four-wheel drive.

The kind I wanted was a used truck of any nature which would get at least 30 miles to the gallon.

As a result, we did a lot of shopping. Finally Tim said, "Dad, there's a place over in Orlando where they sell trucks that have been used by rental car agencies. I understand you can get a real good buy on one of those. Let's go look."

I vetoed the suggestion. I didn't want to buy something which had been rented by someone else.

"Why?" Tim asked.

"Have you ever watched a person drive a rental car?" I asked. "You ought to see them pull out of the airport parking lots, tires squealing, gears clashing. You never treat your own car that way. But for some reason, folks seem to think when they rent a machine they can treat it any way they please."

We finally compromised for a used truck which had belonged to a local fireman. It has oversized tires, roll bar, lights on the top, CB radio, four-wheel drive and gets eight miles to the gallon. Even so, that's better than buying an ex-rental.

When you are a pilgrim—when you are just passing through—you put a much lower value on material possessions. Things are to be used for God's glory, but not hoarded. We are to possess them, not let them possess us. Material possessions are not wrong—but they must not occupy the premium place in our lives. Possessions are to be used for God's glory, not misused for selfish reasons.

Third, one never finds his place until he enters the Kingdom with utter abandonment, slamming the door forever on materialistic and selfish goals as a way of life.

Several years ago, driving through Norfolk, Virginia (in a rented car, of course), I pulled up at a stop light beside a big yellow school bus filled with nuns. Glancing out my window, I saw written on the side of the bus, "Sisters of Divine Providence."

I thought, *That's great. A whole bus load of people living on faith—divine providence.*

Then the bus pulled out in front of me, and on the back door I saw, in much smaller letters, "Emergency Exit."

People of divine providence have no emergency exits. Trusting God means sealing up all the other ways out. It's like those teenager friends of Daniel who said to Nebuchadnezzar, "O King, we will not serve thy gods, for our God is able to deliver us from the fiery furnace. But even if He doesn't intervene, we'll still not disobey Him."

To them, trusting God meant sealing off all emergency exits. And so it does with today's pilgrims. It means welding all the doors shut. It means burning all the bridges so we cannot go back. It means turning your back on everything but the tabernacles of God.

Recently I had a bedtime conference with my 18-year-old son, Tim. He's a very special fellow, as is each of our five children. I was sitting on the side of his bed in the darkened bedroom, talking, as we often do just before he goes to sleep. He said, "Dad, do you remember several weeks ago in church when you were talking about heroes?"

I nodded in the darkness and said, "I remember."

"Well," he continued, "you asked us to make a list of the heroes in our lives. You asked the men to write down the male heroes and the women to write down their female heroines. Then, when we had finished, you asked the women how many of them had written down their moms as their number one female heroine— and how many of the men had listed their dads as their number one hero."

"I remember," I said.

"Well, there were about a thousand people present, and you

said only five of the men raised their hands when you asked who had listed their dad as their number one hero." Tim paused. I waited. Then out of the darkness his voice continued. "I was one of those five."

I was too choked up to reply and was grateful for the darkness.

I reached out, put my hand on his muscular shoulder, and prayed for him. But even as I prayed, I knew there was something greater than naming his dad as his number one hero—and that was finding his place in God.

I am eager for Tim, and all the Tims of this world, to look beyond their dads to the eternal God who is their refuge. Our hearts are homesick for the courts of the Lord.

IV

The Joy and Danger
of Discovery

The desire to belong—to find a place—is basic in our nature. However, the Spirit-filled man will never be content to remain caged, despite the safety that bars seem to provide. Once aloft on the winds of God, the spirit of man is activated to adventure. It will never be satisfied unless it is moving upward—exploring, discovering, venturing.

I am sure this drive for adventure is one of the reasons I have been drawn back to the Sinai on an almost annual basis during the last several years. My stated purpose for these trips was to collect data and photos for a book on the wilderness experience—following the footsteps of Moses. However, when a 47-year-old man, who spends the majority of his time behind a typewriter or sitting in comfortable living rooms talking with overfed Americans, starts making out bivouac equipment lists and then heads off into one of the world's most desolate and remote areas, you can assume that book research is only an excuse. The real reason is to fulfill that God-given sense of adventure which is common to all men—especially those controlled by the Holy Spirit.

Last year, dressed in shorts and Arab headdress, the *kaffiyeh*, sitting crosslegged in the sand of Wadi Feiran and sifting small pebbles through my fingers, I realized I was "home." Yet it was

not the rocks and sand which called me back but the relationship
When God descended upon Mount Sinai, He was accompanied
by thousands of angels—some of whom are still resident in that
place. Moses, the lone figure, clung to the craggy sides of the
mountain overcome by what was taking place in front of him.
Even the mountains around him were illuminated by the divine
glory. Despite the passage of 3,200 years and the constant shift
of political power, that glory remains. And whether sitting in the
sand or climbing the mountains, I somehow seem to be a part of
that remaining presence.

There is within me this drive to explore. It is more than the
spirit of the voyeur: it demands participation—accompanied by
an element of risk. Yet like the eagle, unless one spreads his wings
and soars, he will never see more than the bars of his cage—much
less be able to experience what lies beyond the ranges.

The last trip was made with 12 men in an open, four-wheel-
drive truck which bounced across the rocky desert and through
the sometimes narrow, sometimes wide wadis which wind their
way among the towering mountains. We would often dismount
to climb mountains or, taking our canteens, trek through the narrow
gorges and meet the truck on the other side many hours later.
We cooked our own food and slept under the stars.

Rain in the Sinai is rare. But when it comes, it is an awesome
experience. The water roars off the barren mountains, fills the huge
wadis, and rages toward the sea in a mighty tidal wave of fury
and force. Entire Bedouin tent villages and herds have been swept
away when this happens. The wise guide always checks the sky
before leading his group into one of those dried riverbeds, for a
sudden flash flood could be disastrous.

The third day out we cut inland from the Gulf of Suez and
made our way through a wide wadi, bouncing along in the ruts
of other vehicles which had gone before, perhaps months in advance.
Late that afternoon one of the men beside me in the back of
the dusty truck pointed at the steep side of a mountain on the
opposite side of the riverbed. He had spotted an abandoned turquoise mine, thousands of years old.

"There may be turquoise bits still in the mine," I said.

"Let's explore," the others suggested

I asked the Israeli driver to stop and explained our group wanted to climb the mountain and explore the mines. I asked if he would leave the sandy ruts and drive us closer to the base of the mountain.

He scowled, wrinkled his brow, and shook his head. "No way!" he grunted. "Too dangerous."

During an earlier Sinai campaign, he told us, the Israelis had placed explosive land mines in that particular wadi, knowing it was the only way the Egyptians could escape through the rugged territory. They had kept a chart of the mine placements, intending to return and retrieve them after the war. However, at the height of the campaign, one of those rare cloudbursts flooded the Sinai. Torrents of rain fell on the desert mountains, pouring off the sides of the treeless cliffs and roaring through the ancient riverbed in destructive mayhem on its way to the Gulf of Suez. The land mines had been swept out of the ground and scattered all over the broad wadi. Some had exploded in the force of the water, but others were still buried in the trackless sand. Experienced drivers knew the only safe place was in the ruts made by a previous truck or military tank. In fact, just a few months before, an Israeli colonel had been killed when his jeep ran over one of those old land mines and it exploded.

Our driver said the only way we could explore the turquoise mines would be to dismount from the truck and walk across the sand. But he—and his truck—would remain behind.

"Just walk lightly," he added, slouching down in the seat and pulling his cap over his eyes for a nap. "I'll be waiting here—if you get back."

I glanced at the other men. It was too much of a challenge to pass up. But we walked gingerly.

When we got back to the truck with our pockets full of beautiful turquoise nuggets, our driver said most pilgrims choose to stay in the safety of the ruts. He then reminded me it was "tradition!" which had kept the Jews alive all these centuries. "But," he smiled, "we don't have any turquoise either."

Ruts are safe and comfortable. But Christians must grow. Or die. And nothing is worse than death from sameness.

Growth demands change. Change demands movement, sometimes across the trackless sands of the untried. But to venture from the road and run the risk of being blown up—just to make a new spiritual discovery—well, no thank you; I'll just remain with the truck.

There is nothing more distracting to a denominational program rumbling along in the ruts of yesteryear, or to a pastor asleep behind the wheel of his stalled church, than to hear a group of people on the other side of the wadi shouting, "Hey, look what we've found!"

Just one man in a congregation who decides to raise his hands in praise; just one woman who prophesies; just a small Tuesday night prayer group where the people study the Bible and lay hands on the sick for healing—can cause an entire congregation to stampede across the mine field. Therefore, rather than lead the way, many leaders prefer to chain the offender to the truck—or if he persists, run over him. If we can just still that voice which keeps talking about spiritual discoveries, we can get on with the busyness of our lives.

Most leaders know how to handle a fanatic. But what do you do with someone who is genuinely bent on spiritual discovery, who has as his goal in life to be under the control of the Holy Spirit?

The question, you see, every person must face is: Who (or what) controls my life? For none of us is the captain of our soul or the master of our fate. We are controlled by our senses, our traditions, our habits, our reactions, our feelings. Some are controlled by demons. Others are controlled by the Holy Spirit.

But daring to live the venturesome life of the eagle is risky business. When Jesus closed the book in the synagogue in Nazareth and sat down—after having defined His purpose—the religious people rose up in furor and tried to kill Him. He had threatened them by saying He was leaving the ruts and heading out across forbidden territory.

It's dangerous out there. And sometimes lonely. Yet, as Kipling said in "The Explorer," there is a voice beyond the mountains calling, which somehow keeps us going, pioneering, searching:

Something hidden. Go and find it. Go
and look behind the Ranges—
Something lost behind the Ranges.
Lost and waiting for you. Go!

Thus, despite our timidity, our hesitancy, our proneness to make mistakes, we know there is more, much more than we have experienced in our dusty ruts of traditional religion. The call of spiritual adventure grows louder the closer we move to God. So we venture out.

"Because it is there," said George Leigh Mallory earlier in this century when asked why he wanted to climb Mount Everest. "Because it is there."

As long as I can remember, I have been challenged by people with purpose. Those who dream impossible dreams—and then bring them into being.

A while back, a friend of mine, Bob Burdick, a senior pilot with United Airlines, took his vacation to fly a small, single-engine airplane across the Atlantic Ocean. The Wycliffe Bible Translators in Nepal needed the plane for their ministry. With his teen-age daughter as his only passenger, Bob flew across the stormy North Atlantic to France following the same route Lindbergh used years before. Then he went beyond Lindbergh. He picked up his wife in France, and they flew over the Alps, across the deserts of the Middle East, across northern India and up into the Himalayas to Nepal—flying to the glory of God.

Dangerous? Sure! But there is something inside me that wants to do the same thing. To do something nobody else has ever done— to the glory of God. After all, what's the use of living if you don't attempt something impossible—even if it kills you.

Several years ago I read of a man who had listed 100 things he wanted to do before he died. They were exciting things. Daring things. Impossible things. He wanted to scale the Matterhorn, write a book, go on a lion safari, sing in Carnegie Hall, paddle the length of the Amazon in a canoe, sign up as an Indian in a cowboy and Indian movie. He was 68 years old at the time he wrote the article, and he had already accomplished 92 of his 100 things. They were the things all of us dream of doing but never attempt because they are "impossible."

The late Dawson Trotman, founder of the Navigators, used to set up difficult but attainable goals for each new year. One year he learned to speak a foreign language. Another he learned to play the organ. He was able to do this same thing when he memorized the Scripture—and taught thousands of others to do it—through discipline.

It seems that those of us in the Kingdom, more than any other people on earth, should be willing to discipline ourselves to achieve the impossible, to do the daring, to fulfill our expanded sense of adventure.

There is a place in the Christian community for the dreamer. Most of us dream dreams, however, then put them aside as impossible. Yet God never puts a desire in our hearts, or beckons us to walk on water, unless He intends for us to step out in faith and at least make the attempt. Whether we achieve or not is almost immaterial; the passing of the test lies in whether we try, in whether we're willing to be obedient to the inner call to greatness—the onward call to spiritual adventure.

I think of the people Jesus challenged while He was here on earth. To a man who never walked Jesus said, "Rise and walk." To a blind man who had never seen before He said, "Go, wash in the pool of Siloam and see." To men who had never done anything but pull fish nets out of the water Jesus said, "Go ye into all the world." To all He said, "Put that dream into action."

Caleb, Joshua's old friend and fellow warrior, was such a man.

Forty-five years had passed since Caleb, at the age of 40, had been appointed by Moses, along with Joshua and 10 other men, to scout the land of Canaan. The land of the Sinai was familiar to Moses. He had lived there 40 years tending the flocks of his father-in-law, Jethro. But he had never been up into Canaan. So when the children of Israel reached Kadesh-Barnea, Moses sent out 12 men to scout the land, discover the best paths and bring back a report.

Their purpose for spying out the land was not to see if they could possess it. God had already told them the land was theirs. Their purpose was to scout out the roads, discover where the cities were and draw a crude map so Moses could lead the people into the land promised by God.

The 12 returned with conflicting opinions. Ten of the spies brought a majority opinion.

"It's a magnificent land that flows with milk and honey. But you ought to see who lives up there. They have people 14 feet tall. Giants. The sons of Anak. And their cities have walls around them. We'll never be able to make it. We're like grasshoppers in their sight."

Only Joshua and Caleb had the vision. "There are giants all right," Caleb said. "But we can take the land, for God has already given us the promise."

But the people raised their voices against Joshua and Caleb, and they barely escaped with their lives.

In disgust, Moses withdrew. God told Moses He was disgusted also. He was going to wipe out the entire nation of Israel and start over again with just Moses and a few men of faith—like Joshua and Caleb. Moses quickly interceded for his grumbling, faithless people, and God agreed to withhold His wrath. But, He said, of all the people, only Joshua and Caleb would enter the promised land. The rest would remain in the wilderness until everyone over the age of 20 had died. Then, using a fresh new generation, He would send them in to claim that which was theirs.

It was a sad day for the people of God. Within weeks a great plague struck the 10 spies, and they all died. The rest of the people were doomed to wander for an entire generation. Joshua would be charged with leading the people upon Moses' death, and Caleb was to inherit all the land he had covered on his initial scouting trip into Canaan—all the land from Hebron to Eschol, where the giant grapes grew, to the springs of Ein Gedi near the Dead Sea.

Forty-five years passed: Moses had died and Joshua had led the people into Canaan where they had conquered the land—city by city. Then came the important but difficult task of dividing the land among the tribes. In the midst of all this parceling, Caleb stepped forward. He was now 85 years old, but he reminded Joshua of the promise of Moses.

"Remember what God told Moses at Kadesh-Barnea about you and me," he said solemnly. "I was only 40 years old when we returned from exploring the land and brought back our report. But on that day Moses promised me: 'The land on which your feet have trodden shall be an inheritance to you and your children forever—because you have wholly followed the Lord my God.'"

"I remember," Joshua answered, smiling at his old friend. "I remember well."

Caleb continued. "The Lord has not only kept me alive these 85 years, but I am just as strong today as I was when Moses sent me out. And I am just as eager to take on the giants of Anak as I was then."

Then, turning and pointing at the mountain to the south, toward the walled city of Hebron, Caleb's eyes glistened when he said, "Now, old friend, give me this mountain."

Joshua looked at old Caleb. His face was leathery from the long years in the desert sun. But his huge arms still bulged with muscle, and his body was that of a young man. Caleb was not cocky. Just confident. He was resting on God and had now stepped forward to claim that which had been promised.

"I know the giants live there," Caleb said. "I know you chose to bypass the city when you took the land rather than run the risk of heavy losses fighting the sons of Anak. But with the Lord helping me, I shall drive them out of the land, and they will never bother you again."

Joshua hesitated no longer. Reaching out, he laid his hands on the shoulders of the old warrior, and blessed him in the name of Jehovah. Then Caleb called his sons and nephews around him— the young men who had come out of Sinai and helped capture the land of Canaan—and told them what to do. With a mighty shout they marched on Hebron, drove out the giants and killed the three sons of Anak: Sheshai, Ahiman, and Talmai.

Caleb was a man who answered to a higher authority than military science and tactics. It did not make good sense to take Hebron.

Joshua had figured the odds, said it wasn't worth it, and bypassed the walled cities. There was no sense fighting the giants of Anak.

But Caleb was not content with that. He was marching to the sound of a different drummer. He had been confident 45 years before. He was confident now. The promises of God never change. All that was needed was a man of adventure.

Every child of God has a promised mountain in his life. It may be a childhood dream or vision. It may be a teen-age desire which has now been tossed aside as too impossible. It may be something God gave in prayer which seemed so impractical it was never tried. It may be some seemingly insurmountable obstacle. But every child of God has a promised mountain.

It's easy to be content with the valleys. Ruts have a great appeal. If it's not giants on the mountain, it's mines under the sand. So men snuggle into ecclesiastical gowns, bury themselves in their libraries of musty books, talk about the way things were, recite the creeds, build the cathedrals, draw charts of end times, but never venture out into the arena of the impossible, never taste of new wine, much less experiment with a new wineskin.

My friend Roger Wilson says he is building his life and his family so that if the Holy Spirit were ever removed, everything would fall apart.

That's real mountain climbing.

That's the way churches need to be built: so if the Spirit of God is ever removed, the walls will fall down, the roof will cave in, the money will disappear and all the people will leave.

I have a printed sign, in a big frame, which hangs above my desk. It says: "Attempt something so big that unless God intervenes it is bound to fail."

That, too, is mountain climbing.

The saddest of all people are those who taste the power of God, discover it will change them if they swallow—and then spit. They fear the result of digesting the power of God and are content to live in the proximity of commitment.

My friend Peter Lord, a Baptist pastor in the nearby community of Titusville, Florida, tells his church: "We practice daily what we believe. All the rest is religious froth."

There was nothing religious about Caleb.

As a college student at Mercer University, I was challenged by a soft-spoken southern preacher who visited our campus one day. Clarence Jordan had taught New Testament Greek at Southern Baptist Seminary for a number of years. Then one day he began to realize he could teach Greek the rest of his life—and never put the Kingdom into practice here on earth. Life was too short, he said, to spend it in a classroom—as important as that is. He would leave that for others, but he had a call on his life. God had given him a mountain.

So he went down into Southwest Georgia, found a piece of property near Americus and founded a little community farm. But this was the early 1950s and communal farms weren't very popular among Georgians—especially those where blacks and whites lived and ate together.

Folks in that section of Georgia couldn't handle it. So they burned his buildings. They dynamited his peanut barn. They boycotted his people so they couldn't buy cottonseed, hay or feed for their cattle. Clarence and his people had to drive all the way to Columbus to buy food, and often when they returned at night and drove down the long dirt road to Koinonia Farms, they were shot at by neighbors with rifles and shotguns. They were called communists—for that was the worst thing you could call a person back then.

I sat at the feet of Clarence Jordan all that afternoon, listening as he quoted the words of Jesus about the Son of Man having no place to lay His head, about leaving father and mother and brother and sister to follow, about taking up the cross daily. He was the only man I had ever heard who was willing to die for what he believed. I had met lots of folks who were willing to kill for what they believed—but never a man willing to die. I was 22 years old and looking for a cause.

I know now that if Clarence Jordan had pointed at me and said, "Jamie, lay down your nets, and come follow me," I never would have hesitated. I would have walked away from my college classes, from my planned career, from my friends—to become his disciple. Why? Because he was unlike any other preacher I had ever met. He was not just talking about brotherhood from the leafy boughs of his safe pulpit, he was living it. Even if it killed him. I would have followed him because he was the only man I had ever heard who blew a certain sound on his trumpet. He knew where he was going. And men like that were rare in those days.

Now there are a number of men coming forth who know where they are going. These are men who are unafraid of the land mines, unafraid of the giants of Anak and willing to lay claim to the mountain God has given them.

They are men who have discovered the five-word secret of Caleb: he *wholly followed the Lord God.*

Nevertheless my brethren that went up with me made the heart of the people melt: but I *wholly followed the Lord my God* (Joshua 14:8).

. . . Surely the land whereon thy feet have trodden shall be thine inheritance . . because *thou hast wholly followed the Lord my God* (Joshua 14:9).

Hebron therefore became the inheritance of Caleb . . . because *he wholly followed the Lord God of Israel* (Joshua 14:14).

But my servant Caleb, because he had another spirit with him, and *hath followed me fully*, him will I bring into the land . . . (Numbers 14:24).

No divided loyalties. No murmuring or complaining. Only a steady obedience to light received—and a willingness to wait 45 years to see the promise fulfilled.

The worst of all heresies is to despair of those childhood ideals, those dreams that stimulated us when our minds were still young and innocent. Too many of us have reached the crisis of middle life and, disillusioned, put aside our dreams of youth.

"Too impossible," we say sadly. "Too foolish. Too ambitious. Too dangerous."

On the island of Mindanao, in the southern archipelago of the Philippines, is a small coastal barrio called San Jose. A number of years ago an evangelist by the name of Gonzalez founded a church there. The church grew and a number of people accepted Jesus Christ as Lord. Soon nearly all in the community were Christian, and a school was started. When the elder Gonzalez died, his son Aley carried on the ministry. Aley believed in a God of miracles and told the people in the barrio and church that the age of miracles had not passed. Many believed him and were baptized in the Holy Spirit. Both the church and the school continued to grow.

One afternoon the second grade teacher announced a test. He told all the children to be sure and bring a pencil and paper the next day for the exam. Since most of the children were very poor, they did not ordinarily carry pencils and paper to school.

The following morning all the children showed up with pencil and paper except one. This little eight-year-old, brown-skinned Filipino boy came from an extremely poor family. He lived in a palm thatched hut and had no shoes or shirt—only a ragged pair of shorts to wear to school. He had found a single sheet of notebook paper but he had no pencil. The teacher told him he was sorry, but he could not sit in on the examination since he had no pencil. He would have to wait outside until the test was over.

Heartbroken, the little boy walked out the door and sat on the front steps of the little school building which also was used for a church on Sunday. He remembered Pastor Aley Gonzalez's sermons on miracles, on the great God who did impossible things.

"Dear God," he prayed, closing his eyes and raising his face toward the sun, "please send me a pencil. I want to take the test."

He opened his eyes and looked all around, expecting that God would drop the pencil out of the sky. But there was nothing. Only the shiny white pebbles on the sand, the sound of the wind rustling the branches of the coconut palms and the gentle lapping of the surf on the nearby beach.

His eyes filled with tears as he sat, his arms folded around his knees, his single sheet of notebook paper in his hand.

As children will do, he rolled the notebook paper into a small cylinder, rolling it back and forth between his open palms, tears dripping down his cheeks. Then, as he twirled the paper in his hands, he felt something hard—round and hard—inside the paper.

72

He quickly unrolled the notebook paper, and there in the middle was a bright shiny yellow pencil. It had a brand new eraser on one end, and the other end was machine sharpened—even though there was not a pencil sharpener within 30 miles. He quickly ran into the schoolhouse, waving his pencil. The teacher asked him where he had gotten such a magnificent pencil, and the little boy paused, thought, and finally said, "The impossible God gave it to me."

I was in San Jose the following year, a guest of Aley Gonzalez. I talked to the little boy. He showed me his pencil. He had used it over and over and had broken the lead a number of times and sharpened it with his father's machete. But it was still a good pencil. And there were no other pencils like it in all the barrio.

The reason pencils appear to little Filipino boys, the reason Davids kill Goliaths, the reason unlearned fishermen preach with power while learned theologians often elicit nothing more than yawns from their listeners, the reason old men capture walled cities and slay giants—is childlikeness. They believe in a God who fulfills dreams and does the impossible.

Do not despair of those childhood dreams, those visions which came in adolescence. They are the fiber of life, the stuff which holds us together. Dangerous? To be sure. Foolish? Never.

In the Buckingham home we are challenging our children to invest their futures in things that will cost them their lives—for the glory of God. We are challenging them to go out, even at an early age, and be willing to die for Jesus.

The world does not understand this philosophy. The world says, "Be in control." But God says, "Be out of control." The world says parents should protect their children from death, not point them toward it. But we know there is no glory anywhere outside that which is done strictly for the glory of God. Abundant life comes only when we give our lives totally and completely to that to which God has called us.

As a young man, Dwight L. Moody was challenged by someone who said, "The world has yet to see what God can do with one man who is totally committed to Him." Moody was an unlikely candidate. His English was atrocious. He had no formal education.

He made his living as a shoe clerk. But he had a dream—a vision. And he said, "I'll be that man." Twenty years later he stood with one foot in Chicago, the other in London and shook two continents with the Gospel of Jesus Christ. He had learned to put aside all those urgent matters which pulled at his coattail and do only the important things God had called him to do. He was an overcomer.

The climax of my Sinai excursions has always been the climbing of Jebel Musa, the Mountain of Moses. Rising 7,500 feet out of the desert sand, the magnificent, three-peaked mountain stands not only as mute testimony to our triune God but as a challenge to all who dare ascend its rugged flanks as Moses did to receive the law.

On my last trip, with 12 other men along, we reached Sinai on the seventh day. In order to get to the summit by dawn, we had to begin the climb no later than 2 A.M. Climbing in the dark can be a stumbling, groping experience. Or it can be the adventure of a lifetime. I had hired a 12-year-old Bedouin boy to guide us up the backside of the mountain. I knew, from past experience, that the moment we left the desert floor and our eyes adjusted to the darkness—away from our campfire—there would be ample light to see by starlight. The Sinai is one of those rare places of the world entirely free from air pollution. Only during certain times of the year are there any clouds. At night, once your eyes adjust to night sight, the light from a billion stars provides ample light to climb the mountain. But the first several hundred feet of climbing are the hardest as you stumble over sharp stones and cling to the larger rocks to keep from falling.

After about 10 minutes I stopped our group, allowing the slower ones to catch up as we bunched in the chilly darkness of the steep mountain trail.

"We are going to walk alone," I told them, "rather than as a group. I'll go ahead with the guide. Leave at least a hundred yards between each of you as you climb. Climb in silence, listening for the voice of God as it still resounds from this mountain. Put your flashlights in your pockets. Let your eyes adjust to the night, and you will enjoy one of the most fantastic physical and spiritual adventures of your life."

Having caught our breath, we proceeded up the steep mountain trail, ascending the mountain in the quiet darkness of the desert. The higher we got, the more the panorama of the dark desert spread out before us. The air was clear and cold. And silent. For there are few living things in the desert. None of the usual night noises; just total silence and the beating of your own heart.

I was overjoyed, not only for what I was again experiencing on that sacred place but because of the deeply personal, spiritual stirrings I knew were taking place in each of the men stretched out behind me. Halfway up I paused for breath. I stood in silence, letting my eyes take in the mighty shadows of the mountains, now faintly outlined by the coming dawn. I turned and looked back over a ledge. Far below me, coming up the same path, I could hear the men, their footsteps echoing in the stillness of the canyons. Then I noticed something else: two of the 12 had pulled their flashlights from their pockets and were using them to see the way. Perhaps they had already bruised a shin or stubbed a toe. Rather than run the risk of additional damage, they had sacrificed the beauty of climbing by starlight for the safety of climbing in the small, artificial, yellow circle of light directly in front of them.

I was saddened. These men would reach the summit like all the rest and would join in the magnificent and indescribable spiritual experience which awaits all who attain the pinnacle, but they were missing something of even greater value—the joy and adventure of the ascent.

Despite the glory that awaits all of us when we are transformed from this earth into heavenly places, the adventure of the climb is the thing that makes it all worthwhile. I am grateful for crutches—and flashlights—but I yearn for the time when I can climb without them, experiencing the sheer joy of the Spirit-controlled life.

In 1948 God spoke to a young student at Wheaton College, a small liberal arts college near Chicago, and promised him a mountain—a mountain which would turn out to be a lonely beach on an uncharted jungle river in Ecuador.

One day, sitting alone in his study, he read the first chapter of Hebrews. There, in verse seven, he ran across the phrase: "[God] maketh . . . his ministers a flame of fire." Jim Elliot picked up his journal and wrote, paraphrasing something Amy Carmichael had written many years before.

"Am I ignitable? God deliver me from the dread asbestos of other things. Saturate me with the oil of the Spirit, that I may be a flame. But a flame is transient, often short-lived. Canst thou bear this, O my soul—short life? In me there dwells the Spirit of the Great Short-Lived, whose zeal for God's house consumed Him. Make me thy fuel, Flame of God."

Jim took his mountain and it cost him his life. On January 9, 1956, a rescue party found his body, along with the bodies of four fellow missionaries, floating face down with Auca spears protruding from their backs.

But because those five men gave their lives climbing their mountain, not only have many in the Auca tribe been converted, but literally thousands of young men and women have stepped forward to answer the call of missions and fill their vacant places. And that section of the Ecuadorian jungle, once alive with tiny sons of Anak, is now full of praises coming from the brown lips of the sons of God.

If a man is going to die—let him die climbing.

V

Living on the Growing Edge

When I got married and left home to enter seminary in Texas, I never dreamed I would ever again live in a house like the one my daddy built. In Fort Worth, Texas, Jackie and I lived in a tiny duplex and shared the bath with the landlady and her spinster daughter. Later we moved into a little frame house near the school. Our first child was brought home to that small house with an even smaller front yard with the one spindly poplar tree we had purchased at the garden department of Montgomery Ward.

Later we moved to Greenwood, South Carolina, where we lived in a small two-bedroom house which the church provided for associate pastors. After I assumed the duties as senior minister, we moved into the elegant parsonage—complete with formal living room, formal dining room, paneled den, plush carpets and drapes. It had been decorated by the ladies of the church and was always viewed as their pet project. As a result, even though we lived in an elegance far beyond our means, we never could change anything about the house—for it was not ours. It belonged to the entire church and in particular to a committee chaired by a woman who was the best friend of the former pastor's wife—and who always resented the fact we had moved in with our children. It was a very artificial situation, one in which we could never feel comfortable or "at home."

When we returned to Florida after those difficult and heartbreaking circumstances demanded our move, we were forced to live in a series of rented houses in the little community of Melbourne. Our furniture, which we had purchased to fit the huge parsonage in South Carolina, would not fit into the postage-stamp-sized rooms of the little Florida houses. So much of it languished (and mildewed) in a nearby warehouse. We lived in three rented houses, moving and bashing our furniture in the process until even that which did fit in the small houses was damaged beyond any utilitarian value. Finally we bought a subdivision house and after several years added an upstairs with a big bedroom and writing studio. At last we got our old furniture out of storage. But by then it seemed out of place in our life style, and we wound up giving most of it away—after having paid storage on it for almost four years.

Then, after living in the subdivision house for seven years, I began to feel we should move. It was a strange thing, for we were comfortable where we were and had saved up enough money to pay off the mortgage on the house. The children were growing up and leaving home, and there was no need to expand to anything larger. If we had any needs at all, it was for a smaller, less cumbersome house. Yet, for an unexplained reason, I had a strong feeling we should move into an even larger house—with surrounding property.

It was as if God was requiring of me another venture—albeit one without so much pain this time.

We had arrived at a financial station in life where we could live almost any place we wanted. I was 45 years old and no longer dependent upon the church for a salary. I had become well enough established as a writer and speaker to live on my royalties and honorariums.

The pastoral role I had formerly occupied in the church had been assumed by several other qualified men. My role had become apostolic, that of the spiritual overseer. The council of elders recognized me as the spiritual head of the Body. In turn, I submitted to them. It was a very satisfying situation. Jackie and I had found great contentment in Melbourne, something I had never believed possible in my days of struggle in the crush of institutionalism.

For years I had wrestled with being a "hireling" to a group of people. As a minister I had always been paid by the church. I was controlled by an official board. There was no spiritual privilege which did not have a string attached—a string securely fastened around my wallet. I was told how to live, what days I could take off, how many Sundays I was required to be "in the pulpit," what to wear and what not to wear. Even my wife's wardrobe had to meet the approval of official and unofficial groups within the church. My life style was under constant scrutiny by any number of people— all in some kind of official capacity—who asserted some degree of control over my life.

Now our situation had changed. The new church had grown up around me. In some respects I could be looked upon as the founder. But we had majored on relationships rather than buildings, and I had been able to direct attention away from me and was really no longer looked upon as the "main attraction." At the same time, I had been able to impart many of my own attitudes of tolerance, mercy, love, and forgiveness to the Body. I realized the need to submit to other men and did so because I wanted to— not because I was forced to. Other leaders appeared around me, men who ministered without condemnation, who were filled with love and understanding. Jackie and I had "friends" in the church— people who would die for us, even if we were wrong. There had been occasional friends like that in the past, but like myself they were hamstrung by the unreasonable rules and regulations of the institution. Now we were free.

Yet there was this growing feeling we were to move. Not out of the community, just into a different house. The idea that we were being directed by God to buy a big house in the country was frightening. To me it meant moving beyond personal control of my finances, for despite my comfortable childhood, my father had always been an extremely frugal man; somehow I had grown up thinking that to become very spiritual, one had to become very poor. Therefore we made every effort to hide the fact that we had made money. When one of my books brought in a healthy royalty check, it so embarrassed us that neither Jackie nor I would tell anyone. It was one blessing from God I just didn't want others to know about, for fear it would cause us to look worldly—or separate us from our dear friends who had not made as much.

We found great satisfaction in giving away large amounts of money. We bought several cars for friends. We helped a number of young people go to college by paying their tuition. We made a down payment on a lot for another friend who was struggling to find a place to raise his family. We helped another purchase a house. We gave away large amounts of money to missionaries working in difficult places and at the same time continued to give at least a tithe of all we made through the local church. All in all, we were giving away far more than half our income—yet still living as rich people.

Thus, when it became obvious God wanted us to find another house (I say obvious, for the desire of our hearts was growing every day), we wanted to be very careful we did not buy something pretentious—something which would leave the impression we were wealthy and would thus separate us from our dear friends all of whom were far more meaningful to us than any place to live. For we had long come to realize that nothing on this earth is as valuable as relationships.

We had always been careful to drive inexpensive automobiles, wear department store clothing, and eat far more chicken than steak. We had not employed a housekeeper nor did we hire someone to cut the grass. We did not do it because of external pressures; we did it because we felt comfortable in that life style. Besides, this released additional money to give away—something we thoroughly enjoyed.

It was New Year's Eve morning when my friend, Jim Underwood, came by the house. "I've found your next home," he beamed. Jim had been looking for a house himself and knew we had been thinking about moving. I drove with him out into the country. We pulled into a long, winding drive through the pines. There, sitting on 20 acres of land, was the house I knew God intended for us to have. It was surrounded by towering southern pines and a few cabbage palms. The two-story house was red brick, fronted by white Georgian columns. Behind the house was a fenced pasture and a beautiful two-bedroom guest cottage.

It was a beautiful day. The Florida air was crisp. The sky bright blue. We stood in the front yard, looking and listening. Birds flitted in the branches of the trees. Squirrels chattered and scampered back and forth. I closed my eyes and could almost imagine myself back home—35 miles and 35 years away. And I heard, deep in my heart, the voice of God.

"Take it. It's yours."

Jackie and I had looked at dozens of houses—all much smaller and far less pretentious. Each time we had commented to one another: "It's too big. Too grandiose." I looked at Jim. "What will Jackie say when she sees this mansion and hears me say, 'This is to be our new house'?"

It was unoccupied at the time, having been built only months before and lived in only a short while before the owner—a bank president—was transferred out of town. The determining factor was the adjoining guest house, for we had long dreamed of having a prophet's chamber, a place where we could host those in need and minister to them without having our own lives disrupted.

Jackie reacted as I suspected. "What will people think? We'll be isolated way out there in the country. Besides, it costs twice as much as we want to pay."

Yet, despite Jackie's misgivings, I was certain. We prayed and debated for two weeks. The debates between us grew stronger and more heated. The more she argued against living in a big house which would drain all our savings and would probably consume everything else we would make just for maintenance, the more I was sure God was saying: "Take it. It's yours."

Finally, one evening, after we sat for the twentieth time examining the facts, Jackie used a phrase which sent shivers up my spine. "You are not using reason or common sense in this matter," she said. "It's as though you have no control of this—as if it's beyond your control."

It scared me, for during all those years of walking in the Spirit I had always thought of myself as being a "controlled" person—level-headed, reasonable, well-balanced in spiritual matters. Now

I was being classified by my own wife as devoid of all those attributes I so admired in others and, admittedly, in myself.

"Think of all those missionaries overseas you love and support," she said. "How can you stand the thought of living in a house which is better than theirs? How do you think it will look here in this church if the spiritual leader lives in a mansion while all the rest live in much smaller places? We will be accused of being false shepherds who shear the sheep and live off the proceeds from the wool."

Rationally, I knew her arguments were invalid. We already lived in a house finer than any missionary I knew. The people of our community would not misunderstand; they loved me and would be happy for us if we chose to buy the big house—for they knew it would be open for ministry just as our smaller houses had been. Besides, I was not buying it with money which had come from the church but with money which I had earned as a professional writer. In fact, we had not taken any money from the church for several years. Yet I was stung. I knew that Jackie would submit to my final decisions, but I was afraid to step out unless I knew for sure God was leading.

"We'll move ahead," I told Jackie. "But we'll not sign a contract until all the lights are green."

Our personal friend, Gail Whitley, who was acting as our broker, called early one morning in late January. "Everything is approved," she said. "I'll be at your house at 11 A.M. for you to sign the final papers."

I walked back into the breakfast room where Jackie was finishing her cup of tea. "That was Gail," I said. "She'll be here at 11 A.M. for the final signing."

Jackie reached out and took my hand. "If you're certain, then I'm with you."

I began to pace the floor, voicing my own misgivings. We were getting ready to invest all our savings—plus money not yet earned—in a house and 20 acres of land.

"I thought you said God directed you to buy it," Jackie said. "Why are you now so uncertain?"

82

"It is one thing to be certain when it doesn't cost you anything," I said. "Now, in less than two hours, we will be penniless again."

"But we'll be in the will of God, won't we?" Jackie encouraged me.

I was astounded how the debate had reversed itself.

I sat down at the table and we did what we had done many times in the past few weeks. We prayed. But this time there was no reassuring feeling when the prayer was over. Just continuing doubts. What if I have written my last book? What if the publishing company goes bankrupt and cannot pay my royalties on the previous books? What if all Jackie's fears about the people rejecting us if we act affluent were correct? What if . . .

Confused and bewildered, I left the house and drove to the post office to check the mail. I told Jackie I would be back at 11 A.M. to meet Gail. "But if I don't have any more assurance than I have now, the deal is off."

There was only one letter in the box at the post office. It was hand addressed in a plain white envelope. The return address, in the top corner, was from a woman I did not know in Jacksonville, Florida. *Odd*, I thought, *usually the box is stuffed with mail*.

I stood at the high table in the post office and opened the letter. Inside were two sheets of paper typed with a manual typewriter. The first was a short note of explanation.

"You don't know me," the writer stated. "But three weeks ago I received this prophecy from the Lord and He told me it was for you. I wrote it down and submitted it to my husband and to my pastor. Both of them confirmed it was of the Lord and encouraged me to send it to you. I hesitated, since it was so strange to send a prophecy through the mail to a man I had never met. But this morning God said I should send it. I feel I have now satisfied my obligation and leave the results in the hands of the Holy Spirit." The letter was signed by a woman I had never met—and to this day have not met.

The other sheet was typed, double-spaced. Across the years I had received a number of prophecies through the mail. Seldom, if ever, did they have meaning. This one was radically different:

Questioning me does no good of late, my son. Have I not taught thee to follow by thy spirit and lean toward that which is unquestionable and right to thee? Why have you worried? Am I not God? Do I not own the cattle on a thousand hills? How fruitless is doubt. Henceforth, lift up high thy head, thy hands, sing again thy songs to me, for I am God. I send to thee a word to say only that I love thee with a love beyond what ye comprehend. Surely as I love thee with such might, shall I send to thee all thy direction. Thy concern and worry can ye now give up, for I am God and my answer and direction is even now on the way.

Therefore shall ye further expand the temple, my temple, and be ye prepared to raise a roof of love. Full of understanding and compassion shall be its walls. Call out to my wounded sheep to prepare themselves deeply in my word, for they shall direct lives that have never heard my word until now. From henceforth ye shall expand and send people throughout the country and to lands afar, and fruitful shall be their labors for they have received refuge in your place.

December 28, 1976

I stood immobilized, clutching the sides of the table in the post office. I tried to stifle the sobs but could not quench my tears. They poured down my face. My nose began to run. I looked for a handkerchief but did not have one. I was back where Jackie said I had been earlier: beyond control.

It really didn't seem to make much difference that people were walking by, checking their mail, and giving me strange looks. I wiped my face with my shirt sleeve and read the prophecy again. The tears began again. It was as though God Himself had written the note and stuck it in the post office box. I sensed the prophecy had far more meaning than my relationship with the house, but that would come later. It was the immediate message which overwhelmed me. It did everything but say, "How many times do I have to tell you, stupid, buy the house!"

I made my way home, crying and singing at the same time. Gail was in the living room with Jackie when I entered. She took one look at my tear-stained face and said, "Listen, I love you all too much to get you into something you're not sure of. If God has not spoken to you and told you to buy the house, let's call off the deal right now."

She stood to leave and I said, "Sit down. I want to read you something that was in the mailbox this morning." I read the prophecy, or at least tried to read it, to the two of them. It took me a long time for I kept crying. "On the way home all I could think about were the cities of refuge."

"Like those in Canaan?" Jackie asked.

"I'm not sure," I answered. "But over and over the word 'refuge' kept coming to my mind. And so did the word 'Hebron.'"

"What's a 'Hebron'?" Gail asked.

"It was one of the cities of refuge," I explained. "I've been there. It is located on a high mountain at the edge of the Negev Desert a number of miles south of Jerusalem. It's noted for its grapes."

I opened my Bible to Joshua 20 and read to Jackie and Gail the story of the cities of refuge. Earlier, in the books of Numbers and Deuteronomy, God had told Moses about such cities which Joshua would establish after he had conquered Canaan. In these six cities, scattered all over the land of Canaan, any man who had been unjustly accused of a crime could flee and find refuge. Even if he had actually committed the crime, he could find protection. He would plead his cause to the elders. After they judged him, they would protect him until a certain time had passed after which he could return to his own city or his own house from which he had fled.

Again, as had happened when I read the prophecy, I cried my way through Joshua 20. "We are to sign the contract," I said. "Price is no longer an object of consideration. And we are to call the place 'Hebron,' for it will become a place where the accused can flee and find refuge and healing."

All that we were given that morning has not yet come to pass. I am not worried about it. I am certain—beyond doubt—that God directed and controlled the events to insure I would be obedient. Now, sitting at my typewriter in the upper room of the house, overlooking the backyard, I can envision not one but a number of guest houses. How they will be built I do not know. I can envision a vineyard. And an orange grove. I can envision wounded shepherds fleeing from the wolves which would not only devour their flocks but devour them also, coming for refuge and healing. And I dare not say no to that which God has set in motion.

All that had happened had been a Spirit-controlled venture into the will of God for us; I can only feel confident it will continue to be so.

VI

The Other Side of God

The Spirit-controlled man will eventually take on the nature of God. He will know and trust God because of who He is—not because of what He does for him.

A lot of people have not had the advantage and benefit of loving earthly parents—the kind who discipline as well as encourage. My father was that kind of man—the kind mentioned in Psalm 37 whose "steps are ordered by the Lord." He was the only man in my life about whom I cannot remember having ever spoken a single unkind thing. I loved him deeply and recognized him as a noble, generous, honorable man. By looking at him, I found it easier to understand and appreciate and know my heavenly Father.

Although my dad was the kindest, most tenderhearted, generous man I have ever known, he was also an exacting disciplinarian. Born and raised in Indiana of what my mother called "stern stock," he moved to Florida after World War I and went into the citrus business. He divided his time between his office and his groves—feeling that sweat was just as anointed as a balanced journal. It was hard work in those early years in Florida. Citrus trees were planted and pruned by hand. Few of the roads were paved. The machinery was often limited to a grubbing hoe, a machete and a brush hook. If there was a fire in the woods, you didn't put it out—you beat it out. And you spent a lot of time hoping you would not get bitten by a rattlesnake—or an alligator. It was hot, dirty work, and only the tough survived.

But through it all my dad remained a gentleman. Even though he supervised hard-drinking, iron-mouthed men, he never took a drink himself, never smoked, and I never heard him utter an oath stronger than, "Well, I declare!" Even when he was at work in the groves, his leather snake boots laced to his knees, his dusty khaki pants and shirt soaked with sweat, he always wore his black bow tie. It was his trademark as a former English professor, an army officer and a gentleman member of a society which he believed should consist of more than men with red necks.

He never lost his temper. I never heard him speak a harsh word to my mother or to any of the children. But he knew how, with a well-modulated voice, to let us know that next to the wrath of God, the wrath of a father is greatly to be feared.

Smoking was a cardinal sin. If you can't eat it or pick your teeth with it, don't put it in your mouth, he said. Bad language, of any kind, evoked instant punishment. One night at the supper table, I decided to pull an it's-time-to-let-you-know-I've-grown-up trick. I described a football injury which I had suffered at practice that afternoon as hurting "like the devil." My dad reminded me that any reference to the devil was profane, and I should leave the table. It was great vocabulary training, for it forced me—if I was going to get to eat with the family—to learn to be expressive without being vulgar. Even to this day I refer to my dictionary second only to my Bible.

Only once did he use a strap on me—and even then it was with much forethought and planning. I had been caught stealing money from my mother's purse. It was bad enough that she had caught me with an unexplainably large amount of cash in my pockets, but far worse was the fact I had lied about it and tried to cover up by blaming the whole event on my younger brother. That night my father came to my bedroom, pulled the study table out in the middle of the room and instructed me—with well-modulated voice—to climb up on the table and lie on my stomach. Moments later he pulled up a chair near my face and sat there with the razor strap across his lap. I had seen the razor strap many times hanging on a hook in the closet of the big bathroom with the raised tub—the same closet where my father marked our height and weight once a year on the back of the door. He never used the razor strap, preferring to shave with a safety razor. The strap just hung there like a hangman's noose, a solemn warning that crime was not tolerated in the Buckingham household.

This evening, however, the strap was off the hook, and my heart was in my throat. I had heard my older brothers tell horrible stories of its prior application. Now it was my turn. Daddy didn't touch or refer to the strap to begin with. He just talked. But I heard nothing. All I could do was stare at that horrible instrument of torture—a wide piece of slick leather with another piece of heavy, woven fabric behind it.

After he finished his long monologue, he got up and closed the door of the room—the strap hanging loosely in his hand as he walked back to the table where I was lying on my stomach. He told me to grip the sides of the table with both hands, because, he said, what was about to happen was going to be extremely painful. Of course all that did was tighten up the muscles of my buttocks so he would not have to strike me nearly as hard to produce the needed amount of pain. I do not remember him striking me because, under conviction of my evil-doing and having already seen the instrument of punishment close at hand, nothing could compare with the pain I had already experienced in my mind.

I never stole money again, although the problem of blaming others for my wrongdoing was not so easily purged. That would take years of discipline by my heavenly Father.

My dad, you see, knew how to administer justice in ways to accomplish his purpose. That was the only time he whipped me. The rest of the times he used a similar psychological approach to administer justice. His favorite method was to come home from work early on the days I had been bad. I knew that only a very important issue would cause him to leave his office, and the mere fact I had pulled him away from his desk spelled doom and disaster. Pulling up in the driveway, he would send for me and tell me to climb up in the cab of his pickup truck. Then we would drive slowly around the grass road which took us behind the orange grove to a lonely spot on the back side of the 48 acres. Not a word was spoken. He would stop and turn off the engine. We would sit silently for a long time, both of us staring through the windshield. Finally, when the tension and suspense were so thick I could hardly breathe, he would turn and tell me what was on his heart—his disappointment over my actions, his despair at being an inadequate father, his grief over the way I had treated my mother, or my younger brother, or the fact I had been caught smoking behind the toolshed. It was all a very deliberate—and extremely effective—approach to justice.

Yet even in the administration of punishment, he was kind, gentle, and loving. I never knew him to be otherwise with anyone else either—until my senior year in high school.

I was deeply involved in high school athletics. Especially football. My senior year we had the meanest football coach in the nation. What he lacked in meanness, he made up for in vulgarity. The players hated him and dubbed him "The Monster" behind his back. I called the offensive plays that year, and the nights I got hit in the head a lot, we ran some weird formations. As a result, we didn't win many games.

One Friday night I called a particularly bad play which allowed the opposing team to intercept a pass and score the winning touchdown. As I came off the field, the coach met me at the sideline, shouting vulgarities and hitting his fists on my shoulder pads. Even though he was a large man—well over six feet and a hefty 230 pounds—I was too well-padded to be hurt. I shrugged it off as a temper tantrum and went to the dressing room.

The next Monday after school we were back on the practice field. During a break in the scrimmage, I left the field to get a drink of water. As I walked to the sidelines, I saw my dad's pickup truck near the end of the bleachers. *That's strange*, I thought. Although my father never missed a game, I had never known him to come to practice.

Curious, I walked over and peeked behind the bleachers. There was my father—59 years old, five feet nine inches tall and weighing less than 165 pounds—giving the coach an awesome tongue-lashing.

He had backed The Monster up against the bleachers. Looking up into his face, his finger tapping his chest and the veins standing out in his neck, he unleashed a storm of fury which had the coach pale and shaking.

My little old daddy! I had never seen anything like it. His anger was fierce to behold.

I was scared. I knew, in an instant, what was going on. My father did not tolerate even one word of vulgar language. Nor did he approve of injustice—especially in front of a Friday night crowd which included his business associates. His reaction was to wait patiently until Monday afternoon and then vocally skin this huge coach—much as a top sergeant would dress down a recruit.

I was not afraid for my father. I was just frightened because I had not seen that side of him before.

I ran back on the field and never mentioned it to anyone. That evening at the supper table everything was normal. Daddy never mentioned it to me, and I certainly did not bring it up to him. But always, in the back of my mind, I knew there was far more to my father than I had experienced as his son. To me he was one thing, but to my enemies he was something else.

As I evaluate the character of God, I remember that incident. Most of us have a very low concept of God. We believe He can fail us. We believe we can slip from His grasp and fall into hell— even after He has committed Himself to us. We believe we can offend Him, and He will cast us out. We judge His love for us on the basis of earthman's love for his children. We do not understand His patience, His love, His mercy, His grace, His provision, His protection, His healing power, His glory. We cannot comprehend how He welcomes, even invites us into His presence, despite our sins. There is so much about Him we do not know.

It is good to know one's ancestry. One's roots. But earthly ancestry can become bondage. Spiritually, my roots do not go back to my dad's Indiana. They go back no farther into history than my twenty-first year, when I made a commitment to Jesus Christ and was admitted into the family of God by adoption. At that time my entire ancestry makes a 90-degree turn to the right. My heritage no longer extends back to the native soil of my ancestors in England and Wales. Rather it goes to Galilee, to the Sinai, to a garden eastward in Eden, and eventually to the courts of the Most High God. As much as I admire and respect my earthly father and mother, I desire the characteristics and traits of my heavenly Father even more. As I grow older, people who knew my dad often tell me I look like him. That is a high compliment. But far more complimentary would be to say I was taking on the image of my heavenly Father.

Sometimes I think I would like to go to the doctor's office for a physical exam and when the nurse pulls out the medical history form and asks: "Did your father have diabetes?" answer with a straight face, "No, ma'am, my Father is very healthy."

"Did your father have any fainting spells?"

"No, ma'am, my Father fainteth not."

Of course, I would have to be careful, for not all nurses understand such a lineage. But it's comforting to know—even if they won't record it on the medical history form—that my ancestral roots go back to the Father of all health and that in my blood flows the very nature of God.

As a man grows into the knowledge of God, as he is filled with the Holy Spirit, even his physical characteristics change. The life cells of his body take on the characteristics of the Creator. Even the genes and chromosomes—those unchangeable and unalterable factors in the human body—can be controlled by the Holy Spirit. Facial expressions change. Eyes twinkle. Mouths smile. Sexual drives are redirected. Vocabulary changes. The respiratory system, the cardiovascular system, the digestive process—all these things can take on godly characteristics. As the Holy Spirit takes complete control, we become like our Father.

So it is very important that every Christian establish his identity.

The man who has no earthly roots, the man who doesn't know who his earthly father is, is often a floundering person. I think of that pathetic bard, whose sad poetry and songs touched the American generation of the early 1970s, wandering the earth in his twisted homosexuality, searching for his father. The sad part is, it doesn't really make any difference. If he would allow the Holy Spirit to take control, if he would recognize Jesus Christ as God's Son, he could then join that magnificent family and find his heritage under the Fatherhood of God.

Even though I came from a happy family relationship, there was always a nagging feeling that I was incomplete, rootless, without real heritage until I came into a relationship with my spiritual family—and in particular with the Father of that family. I can share with you the happy experiences of my childhood and tell you about my meaningful relationship with my earthly parents, but it does very little for you. You say, "That sounds like a very happy family. I am glad you had a good father and mother. But that does not help me, except make me wish I had been raised in a home like that."

And that is true. For when it comes to entering my earthly family, no matter how badly you may want to join or how much I would like to invite you in, the door is closed. My earthly father had only four sons and one legally adopted daughter. Now he is dead, and it is impossible for him to have any more children or adopt any others. So I cannot have additional brothers and sisters in my blood family. The ranks are closed forever.

But when I talk to you about my spiritual family—which, in many respects is even closer than my blood family—well, that is a different matter. For my spiritual Father is not dead. He does not even sleep. Not only that, even though He had only one Son— an only begotten Son—He is constantly adopting new children into His family. In the adoption process you receive all the privileges and benefits of the bloodline. In fact, you become heirs of God— joint heirs with His Son Jesus Christ. All that is His, is yours. Through Jesus Christ we can know our Father even as Jesus knows Him, and we can become as close to others in the family as I am with my earthly brothers and sister.

The words of the scripture are so strong in this passage that even most Christians have backed off, afraid of becoming blasphemous. But John tells us that "as many as received Him [Jesus Christ] to them gave he power to become the sons of God . . ." (John 1:12). When we become as He is, then we are not only fashioned into His image, but we become—to a real degree—little

Christs. (Which is the literal meaning of the word "Christian.")

Most of us have stopped, in our Christian walk, with that beautiful confession that Jesus is Lord. We pray to Jesus as our intercessor. We thank Jesus as our Savior. We praise Jesus as the worthy Lamb of God. All this is good and proper. But the highest New Testament truth is not that Jesus is Lord—but that God is our Father.

We don't talk a great deal about that, for it smacks, in many fundamental circles, of heresy. I am not promoting the "Fatherhood of God and the brotherhood of man" theology. We cannot legitimately say God is our Father unless we accept His Son, Jesus, as our Lord. But even Jesus told us not to glorify the Son but to glorify the Father in Heaven. Jesus is not the Father. He is, by His own admission, "the way" to the Father. In fact, He is the only way. Through Jesus we now have the privilege of entering the throne room of the Father, communing with Him, loving Him, worshiping Him and abiding with Him.

That's a bit scary, for to know Him means we run the risk of becoming as He is. I knew, when I entered the presence of my earthly father and asked for his advice or opinion on some matter, that I would have to do one of two things—accept it or reject it. And if I rejected his word, it was the same as rejecting him as the authority. There was no in-between.

And so it is with God. If we come into His presence, hear His word, then we must accept or reject Him. God does not make suggestions. Nor does He give options.

The Bible describes God as holy. If we abide in His presence, we, too, must eventually become holy. But very few of us are eager to take on that attribute of God, for, as Wordsworth once said, "The world is too much with us."

This is the reason any kind of "holiness" revival threatens churches and church leaders. It will require, in the long run, that people become holy, too. Separated from the world. Godlike.

Most Christians do not believe God really controls things. They look at their churches and see they are controlled by men. They see the infighting, the divisions, the jockeying for position, the political machinery, the worldly shepherds—and they conclude God cannot be trusted with important matters.

There seem to be two major areas in which Christians have problems with the Father. One is in the area of *concept and control*. The other arises from the fact we see God as a *characteristic* rather than a person.

Most church leaders have a very low concept of God. To relinquish control of their lives, their finances or their churches to God's Spirit would be the equivalent of mayhem and devastation. Most church leaders, unfortunately, operate off a broad basis of insecurity. Just as surveys prove that many doctors who specialize in psychiatry have severe emotional and psychological problems, so many of those who enter the ministry are spiritually insecure. Their entrance into the ministry, submitting themselves to the rigors of seminary study, the forced procedure of living Godly lives, the disciplines of the church—all are ways of seeking something which will fill the inner void where the Holy Spirit seeks to reign.

I was a prime example of this insecurity syndrome. During the years I was the pastor of a denominational church, I prided myself not only on my self-control but on the fact I was in control of the functions and activities of the church organization. Staff meetings, council meetings, deacons meetings and long range planning sessions were all designed to keep matters under control. As a friend of mine once quipped, we were so organized that if the Holy Spirit dropped out of the church we would not miss Him for a year and a half—for we already had the calendar planned that far in advance. At weekly staff meetings we discussed in great detail the order of service, the location of hymns, prayers and announcements—and, most important, how to begin on time and close the service at one minute before noon. Everything was designed to promote order. The services ran like clockwork. And even though we cast disdainful looks at our Episcopal and Catholic acquaintances who ran their services by the age-old tradition of prayer books and liturgy, we were no better. Everything was always in its proper place.

I now understand such over-emphasis on control was evidence of my own emptiness and insecurity. Much as an insecure father will often physically mistreat his children, so I "ran a tight ship." I was always fearful, although I never voiced it to anyone, including myself, that some outside force could take control and wrest my position—which was my place of security—from me. It was this emptiness, of course, which caused my eventual downfall and allowed all sorts of things to rush into the spiritual vacuum of my life. For despite my attempts to control the outer organization, I was helpless to control my own emotions. Thus, as I began my downward slide, all I did was tighten the outer controls on the church. (This, by the way, has the same effect as tightening one's buttocks just before a father administers the razor strap.) But that, too, I now understand, was part of God's purpose and design for my life. For only through pain and suffering does one learn he cannot control God—he can only submit to Him.

Let me recall an incident which happened during the better days of that early ministry which will illustrate the tightness of control. One Sunday morning I entered the sanctuary for our morning worship service, coming through the side door in our weekly "Parade of the Pious." There, just inside the door of the sanctuary, sat a bedraggled looking man, slumped forward in one of the front side pews. I recognized him as a man I had seen a number of times at the local Alcoholics Anonymous meetings. My friend Ed Seymour, the old alcoholic who taught me "applied theology" the first two years after seminary when I had come to that church, had finally persuaded him to come to a morning service. I was glad to see him, but his presence at the front presented a threat to my idea of what an orderly church service should be. The organ was just chiming the hour. (We always began the Parade of the Pious on the second chime which allowed all the platform personages to reach their proper place by the last chime.) I was last in line, of course, since we always entered in ascending order of importance. Now suddenly I was waylaid as this wretch of a man reached out and tugged at my coat sleeve.

My mind was a torrent of emotions. I wanted to stop and talk, but what would happen if I was not standing at the pulpit by the time the organ finished chiming the hour? I had not trained anyone to take over in such an emergency, so I knew that the entire service would come to an embarrassing, silent halt. I could picture the confused look on the face of the minister of music. He was supposed to lead the choir in the call to worship—"The Lord is in His Holy Temple, let all the earth keep silent . . ." But he could not do this until I had stood at the pulpit and motioned for the people to stand and had read the morning scripture. Everything depended on my being up there to make things work.

Yet here was this man, tugging at my coat sleeve. I wondered, in that instant, if the priest and levite who passed by on the other side, in Jesus' story of the good Samaritan, went through this same turmoil.

"Please, pastor," the man said haltingly, "I need help."

I glanced at my old friend Ed Seymour, who had brought this foul-smelling man into the church sanctuary. Ed was sitting beside him, dressed as usual in his rumpled suit with coffee-stained tie. I loved and respected Ed Seymour as much as any man I knew. He had been sober three years and during that time had not only taught me how to fly an airplane but how to walk into a jail and speak to men behind bars without preaching or condemning. But there was no way Ed could understand the mechanics and psychology of an order of service. He was just an old drunk. He knew how to handle an alcoholics' meeting; in fact, he was a master at that. But he had no concept of the necessity for dignity and order in a worship service. So looking at Ed was of no help. He was grinning and nodding. I am sure he expected me to take his drunk buddy right up on the platform with me and ask the people to pray for him.

But I could not. Instead, I put my hand on his shoulder and said, "Glad you're here, Stan. Sit here beside Mr. Ed. At the close of the service, when I give the invitation, step forward, and we'll receive you into the church."

I turned and moved rapidly toward the platform, arriving at the pulpit just in time to ask the people to stand for the invocation as the organ finished chiming the last note at 11 A.M. Inwardly I was relieved. I had handled that rather nicely, I thought.

But when I opened my eyes after the prayer and glanced in the direction of the front side pew, Stan was gone. He never returned. In fact, he resisted all efforts on the part of Mr. Ed to get him back. Shortly afterwards he was jailed and sent out of town on a work gang. We never heard of him again.

It was unthinkable, at that stage of my ministerial career, to believe God could be so brash as to interrupt anything as sacred as a worship service—or that He might want me, instead of asking the people to stand for the invocation, to kneel and surround this poor man in prayer, allowing brothers and sisters to hear his confession and welcome him into the Kingdom. Even though I was nagged by guilt, I was able to justify my decision to ask Stan to wait until the "appropriate time" to accept Christ. It all came because I was in control.

It was a year or so later, during another Sunday morning service, that I got a second taste of the danger of being in control. The hymns had been sung and the offering and special music were over. I had just stood to preach when I saw, in the far back of the auditorium, a man on the back row with his hand raised. For years I had been running scared in the ministry. Any threat to the routine was a personal threat to me. Just as we did not have a place in the order of worship for people to repent at the beginning of the service, neither did we have a place for people with their hand raised. I did not recognize the man and had no idea what he wanted. Fortunately, since he was seated on the back row, only those in the choir and the people on the platform saw him. He was not causing a disturbance; he was just sitting there, dressed in his coat and tie, with his hand raised.

Several months before we had discussed, in the deacons meeting, what we would do in case there was some kind of "disturbance" in the worship service. In particular we were afraid of what might happen if a black person tried to enter our all-white church. This had happened in several locations across the south in the early '60s, and our local white Christians were afraid it just might happen in our community. Black people were still viewed as mentally and spiritually inferior by many southern whites at the time.

"I don't mind 'em as long as they keeps their place," was the typical answer to my urging to reach out to the black community. Fortunately, things have changed radically over the years and blacks and whites now sit together in many of those former bastions of segregation.

But this man, with his hand up, was not black. He was white—like the rest of us. Yet his presence was just as disturbing as had he been of a different race, for nobody ever raised their hand in our church—even to go to the bathroom. When the initial racial scare hit us, the deacons suggested we install a warning system in the church. This consisted of a button on the pulpit which, if pushed, would flash a red light in the vestibule so the ushers could be alerted to a pending problem.

I pushed the button. Within moments two ushers walked through the swinging back doors of the church and spotted the man seated on the back pew with his hand raised. In absolute control, I waited in the pulpit in something which resembled a dramatic pause, while the ushers converged on the man and whispered in his ear. He immediately lowered his hand, and I began my sermon. That morning I chose not to go to the front door to shake hands with the people as they departed, as was my custom. I had no desire to meet or speak to a man who had raised his hand. It was better if I just let him go out with the crowd.

He did. He never returned. To this day I have no idea who he was. Perhaps he had a cramp in his arm and needed to stretch. Perhaps he was praising God—although, frankly, as I think back about those dead services, I cannot imagine anyone getting excited enough to raise his hand in worship, even a visiting Pentecostal. On the other hand, I sometimes wonder if he was a prophet sent from God. Or an angel. Even so, it made little difference, for we had no place in the order of worship for messages from God which emanated from the congregation. Even from prophets. Or angels. For in those days the Spirit was hardly recognized in the service—much less given control.

Last week I spent the day with my editor, Len LeSourd, in his home in Boynton Beach. After lunch we sat for a long time and chatted. For years Len has been an active Presbyterian layman. Recently he has had a vital part in helping establish a new Presbyterian church in South Florida, one of the fastest-growing Presbyterian churches in the nation. But along with such rapid growth have come problems. Hundreds of them. So Len and I sat, comparing notes between his church and mine. We talked about a lot of other situations across the nation, about what was happening in the big denominational circles.

"It seems the entire church is in a stage of ferment," Len concluded.

I thought about that on my way back to Melbourne. New wine, it seems, is always in the stage of ferment. Bubbling. Expanding. If there is not some outlet, some elasticity in the structure around it, it will either cause the structure to split—or it will pop the cork from the container and go foaming across the floor. Either way is messy. A divided church, even though it may bring multiplication of numbers in the long run, is always a sad situation. And to have a pastor ejected because he does not allow the Spirit to take control, is tragic. No wonder pastors and denominational leaders accuse the "Holy Spirit movement" of being divisive. It is. But it is divisive only if the people—individually or corporately— do not allow Him the room to expand their lives, to push out their old walls of tradition and bring them to freshness of discovery, to lift their sights to new vision of understanding, to deepen their roots into the word of God and to move them closer to God's infinite purpose on this finite earth. New wine cannot be contained by old wineskins. It must grow.

A church will never grow spiritually beyond its leadership—and beyond its pastor in particular. But what should a people do when they have been visited by the Holy Spirit and received a new revelation of the nature of God, only to find their pastor reluctant to move, fearful of any kind of movement which might rock the boat? What if he is theologically opposed to the various manifestations which always accompany such a visitation by God? Or worse, what if he is scared because he's emotionally insecure—and afraid to admit it? Speaking from personal experience, I know he must be confronted. Not once, but hundreds of times if necessary, by the sheep of the flock who are determined to move to higher pastures. However, the confrontations must always be in love, never with the threat of rejection. At the same time, since sheep are priests also and therefore as responsible to God as the shepherd, it is often necessary to gang up against him and push him forward, gently prodding him in the right direction. The shepherd, you see, may be dull and uninterested. He sips from his theological tomes, attends his stuffy meetings, prepares his boring sermons and in general is fed by tidbits. On the other hand, the sheep are starving. But their senses are now quickened by the Holy Spirit. They sense there is new grass on the higher slopes, and they know they will die if they remain in the dry valley. So they shove on, hopefully persuading their pastor to go with them, praying he will one day break out of his stiff structure and take active spiritual leadership, going before them into the presence of God as Moses did with the children of Israel, and returning with a shining face to say, "Follow me!" But even if he refuses to move, the sheep must go on. For they, like him, are commanded to "quench not the Holy Spirit." Sad is the pastor who lies in the dust, trampled by sheep who wanted nothing more than for him to lead them.

The second major problem area in our relationship with the Father lies in the area of trust. We do not trust Him because we do not know Him. We see him as a *characteristic* rather than a person. God is holy, we say. But holiness is a characteristic—one open to much interpretation. Yet we force people into our concepts of outward holiness, totally ignoring the fact that holiness is an inner matter—not outer. We force them to dress like our concept of God, speak like our concept of God, and wear their hair the way we think God wears His. Since God would never be caught dead in a movie theater (unless it is to view a Walt Disney film), then we deny ourselves and our children that right. Since we visualize sex for procreation only, we try to make it as unenjoyable as possible and do everything possible to keep references to that dirty act out of the holy places of our lives. And since God is always fully clothed, we abstain from all remarks about nakedness. In short, we draw up our concepts of God according to western culture (flavored with Victorian morality) and, seeing God as a "holy" God, we try to fashion ourselves and those around us in the image of that characteristic. We remain disdainful (yea, sometimes even

101

a bit proud) that it was the "holy" people who burned the reformers and stoned the prophets.

Others see God as the characteristic of love. Imitating this philosophy, flavored with mores garnered from the cesspools of Hollywood and the New York TV studios, we set out to convince the world we no longer have to abide by the law of God—now we live in a dispensation of grace which gives freedom to love and be loved. This understanding of God begets people who demonstrate on the streets in behalf of social justice, who join marches for "gay rights" and "women's lib," who feed the hungry, clothe the naked, and open their arms to every despicable thing which comes down the pike in the name of Jesus. But their character is so raunchy and their behavior so undisciplined, that even the heathen suspect they are poor representatives of God.

Still others have never seen God other than the characteristic of the stern judge. God is a god who punishes sin—and calls on his children to punish it also. Unfortunately, punishing sin invariably involves punishing the sinner also. Thus while those who see God as justice spend much time fighting liquor-by-the-drink, picketing the porno theaters, lobbying in Congress to have prayer returned to public schools, demanding their civil rights and proclaiming that God's chosen people live mainly in the United States, there is often a great lack of love and almost a void when it comes to an understanding of the true meaning of holiness. In short, they are as difficult to be around as the God they seek to portray.

Several months ago I caught an early morning flight from Tampa to Atlanta. The plane was packed. I had a seat on the aisle in the tourist section. Directly across the aisle from me was a distinguished-looking, miserable-looking man. He was dressed in black suit, white shirt, black tie and shiny black shoes. He had a large briefcase in his lap and was busy sorting out papers as soon as we were airborne. I took one look at him and said to myself, *Preacher.*

Moments later he reached into another briefcase under his seat and pulled out a large Bible—the kind with numerous study aids, maps, and an encyclopedia in the back. He pulled down the little tray on the back of the seat and laid his Bible on that—his briefcase still in his lap.

It was too much for my curiosity. Leaning across the aisle, I said, "Glad to see you reading the Bible this morning." I expected him to take the lead and respond.

"Hrumphppp!" he said, looking at me over the top of his horn-rimmed glasses. He quickly returned to his busyness.

I tried once again. "You don't see many people reading the Bible on airplanes."

This time he didn't even respond. Perhaps, I thought, it was because he didn't speak to people wearing dungarees and tennis shoes. However, I suspected it ran far deeper than that.

Shortly the stewardesses were in the aisle serving breakfast trays. Since every seat on the plane was full, and it was a relatively short flight, they were in a hurry. When she got to our row, the stewardess asked the Reverend Miserable if he wanted breakfast. All he did was glance up over the top of his glasses and then continue with his work, flipping through his Bible and shuffling his briefcase full of papers. I assumed he was on his way to some kind of conference and needed to make notes ahead of time. However, it seemed he should have at least had the courtesy to respond with a, "No thank you, I'm a holy man and I don't eat breakfast."

The stewardess just shrugged and asked the two people sitting next to him if they wanted breakfast. They were an older couple; the elderly man sat next to the window and his heavyset wife was in the middle seat next to the preacher. They both beamed at the stewardess and said, "Yes, indeed. We're famished."

The young stewardess smiled and tried to hand them their trays. But she could not get them around or over Reverend Miserable. Twice she tried to hand the trays over him. The elderly couple had trouble reaching up to grasp a tray. Reverend Miserable, obviously irritated by all the activity surrounding his throne, looked first at the stewardess and then at the older couple. He scowled.

"Sir, I cannot reach the people beyond you. Would you mind helping me for a minute so they can have breakfast?" There was a note of exasperation in her voice. I watched as Reverend Miserable leaned back enough so the stewardess could pass the trays over to the elderly couple next to him. Not once, however, did he offer to help. When the couple finally had their trays, he gave them another scowl over his glasses and returned to his holy work.

After breakfast was served, I got up and walked down the aisle of the airplane. When I returned to my seat, I stood for a moment directly behind Reverend Miserable and peered over his shoulder into his briefcase which was still open on his lap. By that time he had put away his Bible and was doing something with his computer—probably figuring out how many years left before the Judgment.

It's amazing how much you can learn about a man from glancing into his briefcase. It was filled, among other things, with brochures about himself. Interestingly enough, his name was not Reverend Miserable. On top of the papers was a schedule of the conference he was to attend in Indiana. His name was listed as one of the speakers. There was also a little biographical sketch which told which school he graduated from, which church he had been associated with, how many buses he had in his bus ministry and all the places he had served—that is, if you can call such a life style one of service.

I took my seat and remained in deep thought. Here was a man who had been trained from early childhood, through his fundamentalist college and Bible school, and by his present associations, that God was a god of justice. It exuded from him and made him unapproachable, stiff, unbending and stern. When the plane landed, I let him push on ahead. I didn't want to be close to him. Nor, did I suspect, would other sinners be attracted to him.

I wondered, as I walked through the airport, what kind of god I exuded.

How easy it is to fall into the trap of seeing God as a characteristic, then imitating that characteristic to the exclusion of all others. Ministries take on the favorite characteristic of God as taught by the minister. As a result, we have developed, even inside the church, a number of cults. We have the Prosperity Cult, the Deliverance Cult, the Submission Cult, the Praise Cult, the Fall-Down-Under-the-Power Cult, the Water-Baptism-in-Jesus'-Name-Only Cult, the Discipleship Cult, the What-You-Say-Is-What-You-Get Cult, the Suffering-for-Jesus Cult. On and on.

None of these are wrong. None are complete either. God is all of them and more. If we stop at any stage, pause at any doorway of life and do not enter in and take the whole gospel, then we have limited God and created Him in our own image. God is more than a characteristic. He is a person. Like my dad, He has sides I'll never see but which others see vividly.

How desperately we need to know Him as Father, remembering there are more sides to Him than we will ever recognize. To us He may be love and grace. But to our enemies He may be over behind the bleachers, roaring vengeance and causing them to quake.

The prophet Nahum gives us brilliant insight into this other side of God, helping us enlarge our vision and understand there is so much about Him which is incomprehensible.

Once before God had sent a prophet to the city of Nineveh. The first to go was the reluctant prophet Jonah. God said He loved the Assyrians, however, and was eager to bless them. But He could not bless them unless they repented of their evil as individuals and as a nation. So the Lord sent the Hebrew prophet Jonah to the capital city of Assyria to call the people to repentance. They did repent, from the king to the lowest peasant. God honored their repentance and blessed the nation for 150 years. But after five generations, the nation once again slipped into idolatry and wickedness. They became the destroyer of the people of God, the archenemy of the people of Judah. Once again God sent a prophet. Nahum went to speak the word of God to the wicked nation. Only this time it was not a call to repentance, it was a cry of vengeance. God was angry at the Assyrians for humiliating and destroying His chosen people, Israel, and promised to destroy them.

God is jealous, and the Lord revengeth; the Lord revengeth, and is furious; the Lord will take vengeance on his adversaries, and he reserveth wrath for his enemies. The Lord is slow to anger, and great in power, and will not at all acquit the wicked: the Lord hath his way in the whirlwind and in the storm, and the clouds are the dust of his feet. He rebuketh the sea, and maketh it dry, and drieth up all the rivers . . . The mountains quake at him, and the hills melt, and the earth is burned at his presence, yea, the world, and all that dwell therein. Who can stand before his indignation? and who can abide in the fierceness of his anger? his fury is poured out like fire, and the rocks are thrown down by him. The Lord is good, a stronghold in the day of trouble; and he knoweth them that trust in him. But with an overrunning flood he will make an utter end of the place [of the wicked] . .

Behold upon the mountains the feet of him that bringeth good tidings, that publisheth peace! O Judah, keep thy solemn feasts, perform thy vows: for the wicked shall no more pass through thee; he is utterly cut off (Nahum 1:2–8, 15).

Here is our Father standing behind the bleachers with His finger against the chest of the enemy. No more shall they curse and humiliate and destroy the children of God. This time the Assyrians were not just dealing with children, they were face to face with the Almighty God, the Creator of the universe, and His wrath was mighty to behold. Yet that night, back in the Father's house, God had only words of peace and comfort for His children, Judah.

God has two faces—one which is presented to those who would harm and destroy His children, and one He presents to His children. So Nahum is a horrible book, but it is accurate. For in it we see the other side of God, a God of terror to His enemies, who destroys them with His mighty arm and the flame of His wrath. But at the same time, who reaches out in tender mercy to those who would trust Him—to those who would turn to Him for help.

In our desire to discover the person of God, we need to make an occasional trip behind the bleachers and see Him standing against our enemies. Who are the enemies of God's children? Disease. Deception. Sin. Demonic forces. Satan. When these come against the people of God, our loving heavenly Father builds up a storm, and He rides that storm with the host of Heaven against the entrenched forces, and He grinds the seed of Satan to the earth, and He utterly destroys those things which would oppose Him. He is God, and there is no force in the world capable of destroying Him or destroying His church.

There are occasions when I want to step into all the pulpits of the world, to cry from every steeple, to stand on the balconies and stages of the nations and shout: "Lift your vision. Know Him! Do not be afraid He will destroy you. He wants to take over your life and bring you meaning and purpose."

106

We have a great God. We do not need to fear what is happening in His Kingdom. We need to be willing to move out beyond our own control so He can be in total control. God does not have to be convinced to be separated from His blessings. He wants to bless all His people. He wants to bless every church. And in the midst of the blessings, He will protect His children from evil.

Moses came outside the tabernacle, lifted his hands in the air, and cried with a great voice, "Let God arise! and His enemies be scattered!"

That cry still echoes through the corridors of time as the enemies of God are scattered before the mighty power of His Holy Spirit. That is the reason I am not afraid. To be sure, there is tension and stress in every situation. The church is indeed in ferment. But it is a healthy fermentation as the yeast of the Holy Spirit permeates every facet of humanity and calls us to change and growth.

There is no fear when we approach God through His Son, Jesus. God is our daddy. He loves us. He is protecting us. And even though His hand may be against our backside on occasion, it is not there to punish but to direct. His voice is constantly saying, "This is the way, walk ye in it."

And "the way" is always a venture controlled by the Holy Spirit.

VII

Abiding in the Shadow

I was on the middle leg of a four-week nationwide tour, going from city to city to promote one of my books on TV and radio. It had been a lonely tour. In some of the cities I had made contact with old friends who had met me at the airport and chauffeured me around. Now I was coming up on a blank weekend. I finished my last television interview in Seattle on Friday afternoon and was free until Sunday night when I had another TV interview in Las Vegas. Las Vegas is one of those cities where powerful spiritual forces are at work. I had been there twice before and each time felt under severe attack from the moment I arrived until the moment I left. I did not look forward to going back. At the same time, my loneliness was catching up with me. Everyone on the plane seemed excited. Very few people go to Las Vegas on the weekend for any purpose other than gambling, entertainment or recreation. This planeload of people was no different, and I seemed to be the only man without a beautiful woman on his arm. It only increased my loneliness. I had been away from home too long.

The feeling continued after I reached Las Vegas. I called my only Christian contact, but he was cool. Preoccupied. I shrugged it off, rented a car, and decided to drive out of town. I did not relish the thought of submitting myself to the garish temptations which parade the strip of America's best known center for gambling and prostitution. Even though both professions are repulsive to me, nevertheless I did not feel strong enough to expose my life to the spiritual forces at work, especially in my lonely situation. So in my rented car I drove north toward Utah—and Zion National Park.

Ever since I was a small boy and my father brought back little 3-D slides of Zion Park, the kind you could look at through a viewscope, I had wanted to visit. But not as a tourist. I wanted to do it at some season of the year when the park was deserted. The red and purple rocks, the towering cliffs, the high mountain trails all had a special attraction to me. Besides, Saturday was my birthday—March 28—and the park would be deserted. What better way to spend it than walking.

Spending the night alone in a small border town, I rose early the next morning and drove into the empty canyon, parked the car, crossed the little swinging bridge over a rushing river and started my climb up the steep path along the side of the mountain. As far as I could tell, I was the only human being in the park. Even the ranger house at the entrance was closed. Usually there was snow in the high mountains, but this was a brilliant, cool day. The sky was cloudless and azure blue, giving stark relief to the towering red, gray and lavender natural stone monuments. It is the only place I have ever been in America which equals the grandeur and awesomeness of the Sinai—but on a much smaller scale.

I walked alone, breathing the clear Utah air, lifting my face to catch the bright sunshine. For two weeks I had been traveling, going from one city to another, spending the nights in lonely motel rooms and the days rushing breathlessly from one television studio to another, from one radio talk show to another. Then hurrying to catch my plane to the next city. The loneliness which had almost consumed me on the crowded plane and which had followed me as I drove out of Las Vegas to Utah, soon disappeared as I began to talk to God in conversational tones.

I walked for two hours along the narrow mountain path high above the rushing river. There was not another soul in the valley

110

below. I stopped and sat on an outcropping of rock, 500 feet above the floor of the canyon. The only sound was the soft rustle of the wind as it blew among the gnarled and weathered spruce trees rooted deeply in the rocky soil. Starting back, I began talking to God about the deep things in my heart. It made me feel good to confess my flaws out loud, to tell Him of the deep burdens of my heart, to intercede for those dearer to me than life itself—family and friends. Finally, having cleared all the problem areas from my heart, I said aloud: "What I really want more than anything else is to know You. I want to know You. I want to know You."

Then I was quiet. Walking. Listening. Deep in my heart I heard Him respond. "You are not ready for that. You cannot know Me until you first abide with Me."

I felt sad and fought back the tears, so real was His presence. Yet I understood the spiritual principle involved. You cannot know someone unless you live with them. Like Martha, I was too busy working in the kitchen to sit in the living room.

I have many friends in Melbourne and others I call my friends across the world. But I *know* only a few of them. I cannot know a person unless I have eaten at his table, played with his children, entered into his life and his problems. I know a lot *about* a lot of people, but I *know* only a few. That's the reason I am constantly probing, asking questions, trying to get beneath the surface of those I associate with—for I want to know them and am eager for them to know me. Jackie knows if I spend the night at someone's house I will invariably go through their closet before the night is over, rummaging through all the stuff on the shelf, opening boxes and drawers. If I use their bathroom I will peek in the medicine cabinet, open the linen closet and look under the sink. Why? Because I want to know people, and the only way to do that is to get beneath the guest towels and fancy pillowcases and see how they live when I'm not around. You can discover a great deal about people by opening their refrigerator and checking their bookshelf; for what people eat and read is a good barometer to their personality and character.

But you cannot know God by just opening His closet or reading His Book. For God is immortal, and we are made of different

111

stuff. Simply going to church and hearing about Him, taking the sacraments, singing His hymns, reading the Bible—even if you memorize it in its entirety—will not open the door of knowledge to God. That comes only when you abide in His presence. But such a relationship is not formed overnight. It takes a lifetime. And beyond.

The prodigal son—and his elder brother—lived with their father all their lives, yet neither of them knew him. When Moses was on Mount Sinai with God, the Lord told him to hide himself in the cleft of the rock and He would pass by. But all God revealed was His backside. Moses had not done enough abiding.

Nor have I.

So as I walked that lonely mountain trail in Zion National Park, my hands raised in praise, my voice crying out in the wilderness seeking to know Him, His answer continued in my heart, "You are asking for that which you are not prepared to receive. You don't even know the people around you. You barely know your wife and children. How can you know Me? All you can do is obey Me."

Behind me, as I walked and prayed, I heard footsteps. I was momentarily startled, for I hadn't seen anyone else on the mountain path that entire morning. Embarrassed, I quickly lowered my hands and turned around. There was no one there. I could see far back up the trail, and it was empty. Only the clouds, the sky and the magnificent red and purple mountains. I started to walk again, this time reluctant to pray out loud or raise my hands. Again I heard the soft *crunch, crunch, crunch* of feet on the gravel behind me.

Once again I paused and looked. The path was empty. I smiled. Perhaps it was my imagination. Perhaps it was not. I turned and started on down the path, my hands once again raised in praise, my face up, catching the full rays of the early afternoon sun. Deep in my heart a passage of scripture, once committed to memory but long forgotten, came to life.

And though the Lord give you the bread of adversity, and the water of affliction, yet shall not thy teachers be removed into a corner any more, but thine eyes shall see thy teachers: and thine ears shall hear a word behind thee, saying, This is the way, walk ye in it, when ye turn to the right hand, and when ye turn to the left" (Isaiah 30:20–21).

I would never see Him—at least this side of Glory—for His face is too much for me to behold. To His enemies He bares His arm, but His children hear only the soft sound of His voice behind saying, "This is the way, walk ye in it."

The higher way of guidance is not to follow the Lord but to go before Him as He directs. He longs to bring His children into such maturity that they can walk alone. He does not desire to hold us with a tight rein as a horse or mule but with freedom, guided only by His eye upon us. If at any moment we misstep, if our ear is tuned to His voice, He will speak softly and say, "No, not that way, this is the way—walk ye in it."

We need to tune our spiritual ears to the voice behind us.

The loveable Dutch woman, Corrie ten Boom, once taught me something about abiding with God. She was in our home while I was working on *Tramp for the Lord*. One afternoon we took a few hours off and went down the coast to see our old friends, Will and Eloise Orr, with whom she had stayed on a previous visit. After chatting a while, we walked out into Dr. Orr's beautiful yard overlooking the Indian River. We had reached a difficult place in the book, and our personalities had crossed. I thought she should go in one direction, but she was determined the book should head in another. I was terribly frustrated, and in the midst of this bread of adversity and water of affliction, I finally confronted her.

"Tante Corrie, you do a great deal of talking about walking in the light, but I don't see any light now. All you have done is walk over me in this matter. I want to go one way, and you are a stubborn old Dutch woman who insists we go another. I don't think you're walking in the light at all."

It was a difficult thing for me to say to a woman whom much of Christendom revered as not only a living legend but as a literal saint. She looked at me, gave me her old Dutch smile, and shared with me the secret of Psalm 91:1, "He that dwelleth in the secret place of the most High shall abide under the shadow of the Almighty."

"There comes a time," she said, "when you don't walk in the light anymore."

"I do not understand."

"Well, you don't walk in the light when you are walking through the valley of the shadow, right? There is no light in the valley. All there is in the valley is the promise of His presence."

I understood that principle. I knew the artificiality of lighthearted smiles and happy hallelujahs when a person is going through a period of deep darkness, grief or repentance. There are few genuine hallelujahs when all the lights go out.

"Neither can you walk in the light when you are *abiding* under the shadow," Corrie said, looking deep into my face. Then she shared a little gem which has changed my life. "The closer you get to God, the less you understand Him. But the more you believe Him."

Months after Corrie had gone, that nugget stayed with me. We are called to walk, not by sight, but by faith. The man who knows God nominally, who has a hat-tipping experience with Him, who meets Him twice a year at Easter and Christmas—that man can tell you volumes about the nature and character of God. The same is true with many learned theology professors and puffed-up preachers who spend long hours with books but seldom come into His presence. They, too, have much to say about the God they've never met. But come into the presence of a person who abides under the shadow, and all that person can say is, "Shhhh. Be still and abide." He knows very little. He just believes.

You can write a systematic theology, but you cannot diagram God. Neither can you draw out a schematic pattern of His Kingdom. But he that dwells in the secret place of the most High, who abides under the shadow of His wings, does not walk by sight, he walks by faith. And that cannot be diagrammed—it can only be demonstrated.

Sometimes I wonder whether the abundance of books and articles and sermons about faith is not an unhealthy sign. True, the Bible has much to say about faith. But the faith spoken of has no intrinsic

114

value; it merely links us with the Lord. Sometimes the teachers of faith leave the impression that faith is more important than the object of our faith. As a result, many people worship the promise rather than the Promiser. But it is not the promise of God which heals; it is His presence. Neither the quantity nor the quality of our faith matters. What is of primary importance is the object of our faith. To take our faith apart, much as a doctor does to a corpse during a post mortem, either indicates our faith is already dead—or soon will be. The sooner we leave it alone and start demonstrating it, rather than diagraming it, the sooner it will come into being. The young man who is constantly trying to figure out whether he is in love or not, is sure to destroy whatever love he may have—and will surely discourage any young lady to whom he may be drawn or attracted. After all, who wants her emotions analyzed? Emotions, like faith, are to be experienced—not blue-printed.

It is easy to be deceived in this matter. It would seem the greatest believers are the ones who speak much about their faith, who are always preaching and writing about faith, analyzing it, praying about it, exhorting others to have it and bragging about how much their faith produced for them. The fact is, such conduct actually reveals a sick faith, an academic rather than an active faith. That is why God chooses the foolish over the wise, the babe instead of the prudent. Those who trust God most seldom say much about it. At times they seem unenthusiastic, even unresponsive. When approached by those anxiously wanting more faith, they often seem blunt. They live it rather than talk it.

Some years ago our oldest son came into our bedroom one evening and sat on the edge of the bed, distressed. "I don't know whether I love you as much as I should," he said. "I want to love you. I think I love you. I know I'm supposed to love you. But I don't think I love you enough. How much should I love you?"

We had a long discussion, far into the night, and he finally left feeling he didn't need to do any more than he was doing— unless it was try to obey a bit more. The very fact he was worried about his love for us was sufficient reason to prove his love was adequate.

Across the years his love has matured—and grown far more spontaneous. It is now unstudied and natural. And that is what makes it precious.

One does not get love by taking stock of himself or attending lectures. And the same is true with faith. The people who were blessed most by Jesus when He was on earth were the simple people. They had no time for Bible conferences. They did not send Him offerings on a regular basis to increase their faith, they did not spend hours listening to tapes and making notes on Scripture references, they did not repeat various "promise verses" over and over each morning to increase their faith: they simply believed Jesus, walked with Him, and that was all. The ones who missed His deepest blessings were the smart folks who had to analyze everything He said.

Vance Havner, spicy old Baptist preacher, used to tell the story of the mother bear who told her cub, "Shut up and walk!" when he wanted to know which foot to put forward first. It's a perfect illustration of faith. If we waited until we understood, it wouldn't be faith. Faith doesn't wait until things are just right or until things feel right; it just does.

Much of what we call "faith" is merely irreverent brashness. Healing, like joy, does not come from the promise but from the Presence. It does not depend upon our faith but upon His faithfulness. His command to us is not "have more faith." Rather it is to come before Him with clean hands and a pure heart. In this position of obedience and repentance, beyond our own control, He takes control of us—and of our circumstances.

In the tabernacle of Moses, when the smoke from the sin offering went up from the altar, there was joy throughout the camp. However, after the people settled in Canaan, they compromised their obedience, and God said the smoke of sacrifice had become a stench in His nostrils. Obedience, Samuel told Saul, was better than sacrifice.

But that is always the danger when men grow strong, their ministries grow popular and miracles become commonplace. There is an advantage in being a minority, numbered among the persecuted: for in that stance you must depend upon God as your source. It

116

is, as Havner once quipped, only when Christianity moves from the realm of the persecuted to that of the popular that the power goes off.

It doesn't take much to get started if you want to believe in a God of miracles. Just look to Him. Walk with Him. Commune with Him. Read His Word. Occupy your thoughts with Him. And suddenly you're a faith person. It's His presence which makes it all possible.

When I first started writing this book, a year ago, we had only two of our five children left at home. The other three were students at Oral Roberts University. That left our 17-year-old son, Tim, and our 14-year-old daughter, Sandy, at home. Any time you mix this kind of brother-sister combination you have potential dynamite. Our case was no exception.

Shortly after we moved into our big house in the country, Jackie and I were invited out for a dinner party. Sandy was still not too happy over our move out of the city. The sound of whippoorwills, crickets, and frogs did not give her the security she had in the subdivision with street lights, honking horns and a nearby police station. However, we assured her we would not be far away and left the phone number of the home where we were visiting. Besides, her big brother Tim was there to protect her.

At 10 P.M. the phone rang at our friends' house where we were having dinner. It was Sandy calling for me. "Come home!" she almost screamed into the receiver. "Come home, quick!"

I was able to calm her enough to find out nothing serious had happened, but she was, for some reason, terrified. We quickly excused ourselves and rushed back to the house. Every light in the house was on as we pulled up in the driveway. And every door was locked. Peering through the den window, we could see Sandy sitting on the sofa, staring straight ahead, a huge butcher knife in her hand.

She finally let us in and fell into our arms, shaking with fear. "Honey, what in the world is wrong?"

Then she told us what had happened. Shortly after it got dark

117

and all the night sounds were tuned in symphony, she went to the den to watch television. Our son, Tim, who is the fuse on the dynamite, had sneaked upstairs and gone out on the balcony above the den windows. He had taken a bed sheet, let it down over the balcony and then moved it slowly back and forth across the outside den windows. Sandy, sitting on the sofa watching TV, saw the white, ghostly apparition and panicked. Rushing through the house, she turned on all the lights and locked the doors—including the door to the balcony. When Tim realized he had been locked outside, he came down the back stairs and with his finger wrote in the dust on the windowpane, "I'm going to get you."

Returning to the den, Sandy saw the message on the dust and went into shock—calling us on the phone and screaming for us to get home as fast as we could.

It was a precarious situation. While Jackie comforted our daughter I went outside to find Tim. He was sitting on the balcony, doubled over in laughter. I had to admit it was a pretty good trick and chuckled with him. Then I reminded him that if 17-year-old boys were big enough to pull a stunt like that, they were certainly of the right age to be spanked. He didn't think that was too funny, but after a long conversation he understood my point of view and submitted himself to the belt—in Sandy's presence.

It was almost midnight before the house was settled and quiet. Tim was in bed, still chuckling, although his bottom was burning from the strap. Jackie had just tucked Sandy in bed and headed down the hall to our bedroom. I told her to leave Sandy's light on for a moment while I talked to her.

She was lying on her back, only her head poking out from under the covers, her eyes, still moist, looking at the ceiling. "Honey, let me pray with you."

"Okay, Dad, but please don't turn out the light."

"Sweetheart, it's midnight. It's time to go to sleep."

"Daddy, just don't turn out the light. Please."

"Sandy, you know it was only Tim moving a sheet back and

forth. And he was the one who wrote that stupid message on the windowpane. And he's already been punished. Now it's time to go to sleep."

"I know, Daddy. But please leave the light on tonight."

I sat on the side of the bed and prayed with her, then got up and started out the door. "Please, Daddy," she said. I looked back at her pleading eyes. "Honey, I'm going to turn out the light." I flicked the switch and then came back into the darkened room, pulled back the covers on her bed and quietly crawled in beside her. She reached over, put her arm around my chest and whispered, "Thanks, Dad," and drifted off to sleep. She didn't need the light. All she needed was her daddy.

The only thing necessary to stand the bread of adversity and the water of affliction is the presence of the Father. I can walk through the valley of the shadow of death and not fear—for "Thou art with me." I can handle anything incomprehensible, any calamity, any disappointment—just as long as His rod and staff are there to give me strength and comfort.

When Jesus appeared the second time in the room where the disciples were gathered following His resurrection, Thomas, who had not been there for the first encounter, was present. Earlier Thomas had doubted, telling the other men he found it impossible for Jesus to have come back from the dead. This time he could see with his own eyes. Seeing, he cried out, "My Lord and my God!"

Jesus' response to this man who needed proof was classic—and still speaks to those of us who must walk by faith alone:

Thomas, because thou hast seen me, thou hast believed: blessed are they that have not seen, and yet have believed (John 20:29).

That is what "abiding" is all about.

The Holy Spirit is in the business of weaning us from bottles that we might eat meat, strengthening us so that we no longer have to lean on the crutch of knowledge but may walk alone in the power of faith. He wants to bring us upward to that place of spiritual maturity where we no longer have to explain God in terms

119

of systems or formulas, but rather we are satisfied to know Him as our heavenly Father. For there will come a time, said the prophet Jeremiah, when there will be no more need for knowledge, nor shall we need teachers to say to every man his brother, know the Lord: "For they shall all know me . . . I will put my law in their inward parts, and write it in their hearts . . ." (Jeremiah 31:34, 33).

That day is now, as the Holy Spirit not only etches the law of God upon our hearts but ushers us into the presence of the heavenly Father where we may, once again, walk with Him in the cool of the Garden.

My friend, Peter Lord, pastor of the Park Avenue Baptist Church in Titusville, Florida, is one of the few men I know who has designed his life so his first priority is to abide with God. As a result, he is constantly probing those of us around him to realign our priorities. Last year Peter and I joined our old friend Mickey Evans on a three-day hunting and camping trip together in the Everglades. Each of us brought a son to share in the time of fellowship. One afternoon Peter and I sat under an oak tree while our sons wandered off into a deep hammock looking for wild turkey. Peter, who came to the United States from Jamaica, began his usual spiritual probing.

"Don't give me your answers," Peter said. "Just think about them as I ask you five questions."

Peter's first question was this:

Why did God make you? I knew what he was driving at. He wanted me to define why I was here. What was the reason for my creation? What was my primary reason for being on earth? If the primary purpose of a pen is to write, if the primary purpose of a chair is to provide seating, if the primary purpose of a trombone is to make music—then what was my primary purpose for being on earth? I made a mental note—true to the Westminster Confession: "I am here to glorify God and enjoy him forever."

Second: *What is the thing you love more than anything else?* I was tempted to give a religious answer, but I knew better. One of the best ways to test your greatest love is to determine what you can't do without. I have a friend whose greatest love is his head of hair. He won't even let his elders put their hands on his head for fear they'll mess up his hair. I did not think I was that vain. Inwardly I answered: "My greatest love is my family."

Peter's third question: *What is your greatest fear?* Again, I was tempted to give a religious answer about being delivered from fear—but that's just not so. In fact, everyone is afraid of something. My greatest fear, I thought, was losing my family and being left without their love.

Fourth: *What is your greatest ambition?* Deeply spiritual people are always ambitious people. Not worldly or egotistical ambition but an ambition sanctified and restored to its proper dimension. Peter was asking about my goal in life. That was easy. For years, ever since I started writing professionally, I yearned to write a book that would touch the world for Jesus Christ.

Finally, Peter asked: *Why do you want God?* That took more thinking than the rest. He was asking, in essence, what I expected to gain by being a Christian. That was easy: I wanted God so He could help me accomplish my goal for Him—for without Him I was nothing.

All my answers seemed sound. At least I seemed to have my spiritual pyramid down pat: God first, family next, career last.

"If your answer to question number one is not the same as your answer to question number four, you are a mixed-up person," Peter said matter-of-factly.

He continued. "If God made you to harvest apples, and you are busy planting oranges, you are going to be confused when it comes time to pick the fruit."

"But I said my reason for being on earth was to glorify God and enjoy Him forever," I said.

"That's fine," Peter answered. "Then your greatest ambition better be to glorify God and enjoy Him forever."

But I had not said that. I had said my ambition was to do something for Him, rather than to abide in Him—to have fellowship with Him. Slowly it dawned on me. I am here on this earth for no other reason but to have communion with Him and to renew that wonderful relationship that took place in the Garden of Eden when Adam walked alone with God in the cool of the evening.

121

If I have any ambition other than that, I am missing God's purpose for my life. If I have been placed on this earth to abide in God, then my greatest ambition should be to have fellowship with Him.

Peter continued: "Your answer to question number two ought to be the same as your answer to question number three."

Again I was trapped. I had the right sequence, but the wrong answers. If my purpose for being on earth is to abide in God, then my greatest love should be the person of the Father—not my wife, children or my ministry. Likewise, my greatest fear should be the fear of losing that precious fellowship with God. Paul said that was the thing he feared most, that after preaching the Gospel, he himself might become shipwrecked and lose fellowship with God. He had seen it happen in a number of his associates. "For Demas," he said, "hath forsaken me, having loved this present world . . ." (2 Timothy 4:10). King David prayed so eloquently in Psalm 51, "Cast me not away from thy presence; and take not thy holy spirit from me." If God has placed us on earth to have fellowship with Him and to abide in Him, then our greatest love must be for Him, and our greatest fear should be losing that fellowship.

"I will not ask you how you answered question five," Peter said. "But if you said you wanted God for any other reason than the fact He *is* God, then you are a materialist and an idolator."

He needed to say no more. I was cut to the bone. I had said I wanted God to help me accomplish something I wanted to do for Him—notably, to write a book for which He would get the glory, and I would get the money. That put me in the position of the bomber pilot in World War II who coined the slogan: "God is my co-pilot." Yet I don't want to fly with a man who has God in the co-pilot's seat. I want to fly with a fellow who is co-pilot to God. Too long I had been in the position of giving orders to God, telling Him to go and fetch, so to speak. As I look back over my life and all its problems, I see they all began when I saw myself flying in the captain's seat—with God relegated to crew status or perhaps strapped in a passenger's seat (first-class section, of course). In fact, there had been times when I had taken off without Him, telling Him I would be back in a few hours (or however long it would take to fulfill my selfishness) and would renew acquaintances then.

Many people want God in order to be healed, to be happy, to get out of debt. Others, like myself, may want Him to help out in their ministry. All are unworthy and secondary motives. I must want Him because He is God.

Why do I want my wife? Because she is a good cook? A good mother? A good sex partner? Because she scratches my back when it itches, washes my dirty underwear, answers the phone, gets me out of trouble? But what if she were physically incapacitated? Would I want her then? Not if my reasons were any of the above. I must want her because she is my wife. And so with God.

I have grown cautious about giving God directions—even directions to heal, mend broken families, help folks with finances or give them power for ministry. For years I looked upon God as my servant, my helper, rather than my Lord. I asked His help with various projects rather than submitting myself to His will. I gave Him directions, and I had even been guilty of shouting His promises back at Him in an attempt to blackmail Him into action—when I should have been prostrating myself before Him in grateful submission.

There is nothing wrong with recounting the promises of God when we pray. But we need to remember it is not God who forgets—it is we who have forgotten the promises. Thus mentioning the promises of God when we pray is for *our* benefit—not His. God is not a servant for us to order around. He is Lord of the universe and we bow before Him. He controls our lives and we must want Him because He is—and for no other reason.

My old friend and first publisher, Dan Malachuk, introduced me to Kathryn Kuhlman back in 1969. She was searching for someone to write her second book. I had just finished *Run Baby Run* and had become intrigued by the uniqueness of this woman evangelist whose methods were so radically different from my own. After several days together, she invited me to stay over in Pittsburgh and attend her regular Friday morning "miracle service" at the Carnegie Library on Pittsburgh's north side. It was one of the most mind-boggling experiences of my life. I arrived a full three hours before the service was to start, and there were already thousands of people thronging the doors, packing the steps of the building and blocking the street. After the doors opened and the people pushed inside, there were still a thousand people left outside trying to get in.

It must have been this way when Jesus walked through Galilee, I thought, as I noticed the sick, the lame and the crippled who had come hoping to be healed. I was able to squeeze inside the building and lean against the back wall of the auditorium. The room was packed, including the balconies. The sick were mingled with the well. It was my first time, ever, to be in such a meeting, and I was almost overwhelmed by the press of humanity—and by the awesome sense of faith and expectancy which permeated the room. Coming from a Baptist heritage where not only were miracles and healings relegated to the first century but where women preachers were strictly forbidden, this first service was a deep, soul-shattering experience.

I wanted to believe it was true. I wanted to believe that God still healed as He did when Jesus was here. I wanted to believe all those words I had been reading in the Bible, words which only recently had come alive to me following my own personal encounter with the Holy Spirit. But there was so much doubt. Yet how could I deny these people? I had already spoken to several who gave dramatic testimony of healings at previous services. Nothing could keep them away ever again. And how could I defend my old position where the pews were half empty and the people half dead, compared to the life and vitality that flooded that room?

There was a man standing next to me in a police captain's uniform. About halfway through the three-hour service, Miss Kuhlman pointed toward the back of the auditorium and said, "The Holy Spirit is moving in great power back there." This burly policeman, who had been standing at attention through the entire service, gave a little gasp and fell to the floor. I thought he had died, but the people around us simply raised their hands and started saying things like, "Praise the Lord! Hallelujah!" Later I discovered the reality of the experience of being "slain by the Holy Spirit"

124

myself. But that morning it was awesome, breathtaking. The policeman slowly climbed back to his feet, his lips moving in quiet praise, and took his stance beside me.

Even as I was watching all this take place around me, I noticed nearby a beautiful young black-haired woman standing against the side wall. She was holding a small child in her arms, perhaps eight or nine months old. The child had a horribly deformed head. I could not tell whether the baby was a boy or girl, for the head was almost twice normal size. I tried to pull my eyes away from the pathetic sight of the beautiful mother and her small child, but I could not. I began to pray, *Oh, God, please heal that child. God, if you don't do anything else in this meeting, I pray you heal that child.*

Then I did something I have long since regretted. I began to bargain with God. Murmuring half out loud, I prayed, "Lord, if you will heal that child, I will stand on every street corner in America and speak of your greatness. I will tell strangers. I will go into the churches. I will write books. I will proclaim for all the world to hear that you are a God who still does miracles. Please, Lord, let me see it with my eyes so I may believe."

For the rest of the service my eyes were fixed on that tiny baby, its head lolling on the mother's shoulder. Occasionally I would catch my breath as I thought I saw the head shrinking in size. I was prepared to shout, even prepared to fall prostrate to the floor as the policeman had done. But it did not happen. The service closed, and the mother took her child and made her way through the crowd until she was lost from sight.

It took me months to recover from that. I had laid my life on the line, as seriously as I had ever done before. I had made God a promise. It took me a long time to realize that man is not allowed to make conditional promises to God. Instead, God makes conditional promises to man. It is God who tells us, "If you will, then I will . . ." Not we who tell Him. It slowly became apparent to me that God could have let me see that miracle—and I have seen many since that time—and then I would have gone out and become His spokesman. But how much better to go out and tell the world about God's power, about His ability to control lives, when I have not seen but only believed. How much better to walk by faith rather than by sight. How much better to abide in Him and let the signs and wonders follow—as He deems fit.

I am not a healer, although I have seen people healed. I am not a miracle worker. But I have seen miracles. Many of them. But it no longer bothers me when I pray for someone to be healed, and they are not. The older I grow, the less I know. But I love Him. And I am available. The results—and the glory—belong to Him.

All God requires is that I become a seed that falls into the ground and dies.

> But you will not mind the roughness nor the steepness of the way,
> Nor the chill, unrested morning, nor the searness of the day;
> And you will not take a turning to the left nor to the right,
> But go straight ahead, nor tremble at the coming of the night,
> For the road leads home.
>
> Author Unknown

VIII

How to Let Your Dreams Come True

Be delighted with the Lord. Then He will give you all your heart's desires (Psalm 37:4, TLB).

Edwin Markham once said, that everything in which we glory was once a dream. Everyone has at least one basic dream—something you believe God has laid on your heart, something that has not yet come to pass, but which you fervently believe will happen one day.

All great things are born in dreams. Art. Music. Architecture. Family. Relationships. Even books. All started with a hope, a glint in the eye, a desire in the heart. To the believer whose life has moved into the Spirit's control, the fulfillment of dreams is a profound venture.

Some have already experienced the realization, the fulfillment of their dream. They are the happy ones. The Bible is filled with stories of happy people. These are people who, despite their hardships and sufferings, realized happiness by the fulfillment of their dreams. Hannah was a mother without children who dreamed and prayed for a child. She was ridiculed not only by her husband, Elkanah, but by the priest Eli. But her dream came true, and she gave the world Samuel. Ruth lost the husband of her youth and found herself in a strange land, forced to glean from the fields in order to live. But her desire for a man to love was fulfilled in Boaz, and that union produced men like Jesse and David and finally the Messiah Himself. The Apostle Paul, beaten, imprisoned, condemned to death, wrote back to his friend Timothy that not only had he fought a good fight, but all his dreams had been fulfilled. He was a happy man. And I love to picture old Simeon. For years he had come to the Temple in Jerusalem believing he would see the Savior of Israel. Then on a day like all other days, he suddenly looks up and sees a young teen-age mother holding an eight-day-old baby in her arms, awaiting her turn to have the baby circumcised. And Simeon approaches in awe, reaches out gently, and whispers for only Mary to hear: "Mine eyes have seen thy salvation . . . a light to lighten the Gentiles, and the glory of thy people Israel" (Luke 2:30, 32). His dream had come true.

But to most of us the fulfillment of our dream is still far off. My friend and fellow elder, Herman Riffel, says happy people are those who know they are at least moving toward the fulfillment of their dream. The unhappy, frustrated ones are those who feel their dream has passed them by or that what they long for is impossible. They are the ones who believe life is only a cruel trick, designed to make a mockery of the desires of our heart.

All great men have had their dreams, for dreams are the stuff of which life is made. Take the dreamers out of our civilization, and the entire structure of history tumbles to the ground.

Joseph was a dreamer. Despite his foolishness, his dreams finally came to pass. Moses dreamed of freedom for his people. Joshua dreamed of a nation under government. Isaiah dreamed of a suffering Messiah—750 years before the event came to pass. Peter dreamed on a housetop and the Gospel was given to the Gentiles Paul dreamed at Troas, and the message of Christ was carried to the mainland of Europe. Columbus dreamed. Galileo dreamed. Edison dreamed. Pasteur dreamed. Firestone, Henry Ford, Wilbur and Orville Wright, and Martin Luther King—all dreamed. Markham was right: all that we glory in was once a dream.

The dreams God places in our hearts are all attainable. Grace is the supernatural power which God gives the believer to accomplish His will, to bring those dreams to pass. This is difficult for us to grasp, for we have been conditioned to believe that if we do not bring a thing to pass in our own strength, it will not come to pass. But if we are the living, breathing, acting, loving extension of the man Jesus Christ in the world today, then the things He did, we can do also. His mission is now our mission; His dream, ours.

There are two kinds of dreams: those we dream up ourselves which are nearly always self-centered, and those God places in our hearts. God gives each one of us the desire to accomplish His will, to fulfill the dreams He places in our hearts—and the power to do it. But the only legitimate dreams are the ones God places in our hearts.

The Holy Spirit accomplishes His work in this world by the measure of faith each man is given to express his personal spiritual gift. It is the process He uses to make the dreams He has placed in our hearts come true. This is best understood when we realize that *our loving God has created each one of us to do best that which we enjoy doing.* A number of years ago, I determined the best way to make this principle effective in my own life was to find the one thing I enjoy doing more than any other, then figure out a way to get people to pay me for doing it. In my case, that is what I am doing right now—writing a book. In your case it may be something else. Whatever it is, the Potter has designed something into each one of us which needs to be sanctified, some special gift which when discovered and put into use, will bring you happiness and satisfaction by fulfilling the desire of your heart.

The tragedy that surrounds most people is they are never able to do the thing they are gifted to do. A woman with great artistic talent winds up doing secretarial work in a law office—and painting only on the weekends. A man with a gift as a mechanic satisfies his guilt by going into the ministry. Forced by circumstances, misguided by prior educational direction, guilt or some kind of financial pressure, most of God's children never exercise their faith enough to do the thing they are called to do—the thing they are gifted to do. As a result, they live frustrated lives because their dream can never come true.

However, when a Christian is doing that which he is called to do, that which he is gifted to do, there is tremendous motivation and joy in his life.

If we are privileged to do the very things Christ did, to dream His dreams and see them fulfilled, then we must find out how He did what He did, for herein lies the secret of our own personal happiness.

The best place to start with this revelation is at the beginning of Jesus' personal ministry. He called 12 disciples, commissioned them and gave them "power against unclean spirits, to cast them out, and to heal all manner of sickness and all manner of disease." He told them "as ye go, preach, saying, The kingdom of heaven is at hand. Heal the sick, cleanse the lepers, raise the dead, cast out devils: freely ye have received, freely give" (Matthew 10:1, 7–8).

Later in Matthew 28, Jesus gave His disciples a final commission:

All power is given unto me in heaven and in earth. Go ye therefore, and teach all nations, baptizing them in the name of the Father, and of the Son, and of the Holy Ghost; teaching them to observe all things . . . I have commanded you; and lo, I am with you alway, even unto the end of the world (Matthew 28:18–20).

The commission of Matthew 28 is simply an enlargement of the commission in Matthew 10. The first commission was to go to the "house of Israel." The second commission took in the entire world. However, the purpose was identical. John quotes Jesus' enlarged plan: "He who believes in me will also do the works that I do; and greater works . . . will he do, because I go to my Father" (John 14:12, RSV).

For years this bothered me, not because I did not believe it, but because I did not see it in practice. How could I do "greater works" than Jesus? Now, however, I understand Jesus was not referring to greater in kind but greater in degree. He was speaking of the fulfillment of the dream He had placed within my heart.

As a child I used to dream how wonderful it would be to speak to a sick person, saying: "In Jesus' name, be healed." But I was afraid to try—afraid I would fail in my task and the word would get around that I had made a fool of myself. Now, however, I have not only had my eyes opened to the possibility of this, but there have been times when I have been infused with such power from the Holy Spirit that these things have literally happened.

Several years ago I was invited back to my alma mater, Mercer University, to speak in chapel. Mercer is a Southern Baptist University, under the auspices of the Georgia Baptist Convention. Since I had become involved in the charismatic movement, and my church had been voted out of official Baptist membership, I had felt totally ostracized by most of my Baptist brethren. The invitation, then, to return and speak in chapel was a distinct honor. At the same time I was frightened. The evening before I was to fly to Macon, Georgia, I attended a small prayer group in Melbourne and asked the people to pray for me. During that prayer time a young housewife prophesied: "Do not prepare what you are to say. I will give you the words when you arrive."

That really terrified me. Even though I had been preaching without a manuscript for several years, this was one time I wanted to go fully prepared. After all, I would be standing in front of many of my old college professors. If ever I needed to make an impression for the Lord, this was the time. Yet, deep inside, I felt the prophecy came from God. I determined to walk it out.

Being told specifically not to do something is like telling a man not to think of a green-eyed monkey. It stirs every kettle of imagination. On the plane from my home in Melbourne all the way to Macon, I had to do fierce battle with my desire to let my mind run ahead and plan. At least my first sentence. At least the general topic. But I was determined to obey what I knew was the voice of God, no matter how hard or impractical it seemed.

That morning, when I stepped on the stage of the chapel and looked out over the student body and the solemn faces of the professors, I felt a strange peace. Following the introduction, I walked to the podium, opened my mouth and to my horror heard myself say, "I am a former Southern Baptist preacher who now speaks in tongues."

It was the best opening sentence I've ever given. From that

moment on, every ear was tuned—some to criticize, some to drink in what I said like water pouring from a cracked rock in the middle of a desert. The great and profound things I imagined I might say did not come forth. Instead, I simply shared my testimony.

At the end of the chapel period, a pale young man approached me as I stood in the aisle near the front of the auditorium. He seemed especially frail, his eyes sunk deep in his head, his hair silky and thin. He talked in a coarse whisper.

"I have leukemia," he said. "My older brother died of the same disease at the age of 19. The doctors have told me I would not live any longer than he. I am now that same age. Everyone I know tells me I am going to die. You are the first man I have ever heard who said God still heals. If you believe what you said this morning, will you pray that I may be healed?"

"I will do it now," I said, forgetting that the large crowd standing in the chapel had grown totally silent. Every eye, students and professors alike, was on us. I reached out, laid my hand on the clammy forehead of the emaciated young man and began to pray. I felt him staggering. Suddenly his knees gave way and he began to slump. I grabbed him under the arms and lowered him to the floor. There was not a sound from those standing around, although I am certain they had never seen anything like that.

For that matter, neither had I. For an instant I wondered if the boy had died. But I knelt beside him, and his eyelids were fluttering. He finally opened them, gave me a crooked smile and said softly, "I'm okay. I don't know what happened, but I'm okay."

I breathed an inner sigh of relief, helped him to his feet and stood there as he embraced me, tears running down his face. "Am I healed?" he asked me.

I answered him honestly, not with some formula but out of my heart. "I don't know. That's God's business. But I do know we have done what He has asked us to do. The rest is up to Him."

The boy picked up his books and slowly made his way, walking with a decided staggering gait, out the side door. I made my way through the group of students, who backed off to let me through, to a friend who was waiting outside to take me to lunch. The entire affair was never mentioned—not then, not ever again.

Two years later I was speaking at a Full Gospel Business Men's Fellowship meeting in Cocoa Beach, Florida, a small community a few miles up the east coast from my home. During the course of my message, I found myself telling the story—for the first time—of the incident at Mercer. Afterwards a handsome couple came quickly to the front of the room and embraced me fervently. Gradually they choked out their story. They were the parents of that young man. He had been completely healed of his leukemia and was, according to them, the picture of health. They were vacationing in the area, heard I was to speak, and made a special trip to the meeting. They had no idea I would tell that story, nor do I know why I told it, except to prove once again the greatness of God and to point out that those deep dreams of childhood do, indeed, come true.

We are the expansion of Jesus' mission in the 20th century, and, equally important, we are the fulfillment of the dream He has put within our hearts.

What does this mean—the expansion of His mission? To fully understand what is meant by the continuing and enlarging work of Jesus here on this earth, we need to look at the opening words of the Acts of the Apostles: "In the first book . . ." Luke wrote—and here he was referring to his Gospel—"I have dealt with all that Jesus began to do and teach . . ." (Acts 1:1, RSV). Give special attention to the words, "all that Jesus began to do and teach." The implication is that Luke's second book, The Acts, is a record of what Jesus *continued* to do and teach. Thus, even though the book is labeled "The Acts of the Apostles," a far more accurate title would be "The Acts of the Holy Spirit" or "The Continuing Acts of Jesus Christ on This Earth."

Luke points out it was "the Lord" who added to the church day by day (Acts 2:47). And when the lame man at the Beautiful Gate of the Temple was healed, Peter specifically points out that the disciples had nothing to do with the healing. ". . . why do you stare at us, as though by our own power or piety we had made him walk?" (Acts 3:12, RSV). Then there was that healing at Lydda. Aeneas had been bedridden, paralyzed, for eight years. Peter said to him, "Aeneas, Jesus Christ heals you" (Acts 9:34, RSV). Peter meant that literally. Jesus Christ was alive and at work in Lydda.

This of course presents a real problem to the rationalist or the humanist. It is difficult enough to believe that Jesus performed miracles when He was on earth. But how can He be alive and at work in all ages and in all places? Yet the very heart of the Gospel is the continuing ministry of Jesus Christ through His Body—the church—here on earth in exactly the same way, only greater than the ministry He had when He was incarnate in the flesh.

John the Baptizer appeared at the beginning of our Lord's public ministry, preparing the way. "After me comes he who is mightier than I," John said in one of his public addresses. "I have baptized you with water; but he will baptize you with the Holy Spirit" (Mark 1:7–8, RSV). Shortly after that, John spotted Jesus on the banks of the river and cried out, "Behold the lamb of God who takes away the sin of the world" (John 1:29, RSV). Then Jesus submitted to John's baptism.

> And when he came up out of the water, immediately he saw the heavens opened and the Spirit descending upon him like a dove . . . (Mark 1:10, RSV).

Jesus' baptism was composed of two parts: baptism in water and the descent of the Spirit. The term "baptized in the Spirit" also describes the second part, since those words are often connected with baptism when it is mentioned elsewhere in the New Testament. In fact, baptism in the New Testament is always related to both aspects—water and Spirit.

Now why Jesus needed to be baptized in the Holy Spirit remains a great mystery. For centuries the church has argued the point. But it seems even the Son of God was incomplete. His dreams could not come true without the fulfilling power of the third person of the Trinity—the Holy Spirit.

Jesus' baptism was the beginning of three years of intense conflict. Listen to the way Luke introduces the beginning of Jesus' ministry:

134

"And Jesus returned [from the wilderness] in the power of the Spirit into Galilee . . ." (Luke 4:14, RSV). From there He went to Nazareth, His home town, and on the sabbath day went to the synagogue. During the allotted time, He stood with the scroll and read from Isaiah: "The Spirit of the Lord is upon me . . ." (Isaiah 61:1; Luke 4:18). Then He said the prophecy had just come true and sat down.

The people, who were frustrated because their dreams never came true, were angry at the man who seemed fulfilled. They would have killed Him on the spot but He escaped, withdrew to the seashore, called His disciples and began the ministry which we are called to continue—a call which still bubbles in the hearts of all Christians in the form of their dreams.

It is this dream which Paul talks about in 1 Corinthians 12. He says, "Now concerning spiritual gifts, brethren, I do not want you to be uninformed" (12:1, RSV). The verse could just as well be translated, "I do not want you uninformed about those who bear the marks of the Spirit."

Jesus exhibited the marks of the Spirit. In fact, all that He did can be summed up in the first seven of the nine manifestations listed in 1 Corinthians 12:8–10. These manifestations are also called graces—coming from the Greek word *charis*. We have added "ma," meaning a charisma is actually a "gracing"—the visible evidence of God's grace in our lives. It is all from the Spirit and by the Spirit. Such was our Lord's ministry before His ascension; such is His continuing ministry after His ascension in and through those of us who are now walking in the Spirit. In short, we are the continuing ministry of Jesus on earth.

Jesus was limited to one body and further limited to one era of history. How, His disciples wondered, could He overcome these limitations and acquire universal extension of His presence and power? The answer is through generation after generation of men and women who are filled with the same Spirit who filled Jesus at His baptism. It is God's divine plan for us to receive His Spirit and thereby overcome the physical and geographical and chronological limitations placed on Jesus—and thus extend Him into the entire world of all generations.

135

In John 15, Jesus Himself speaks the word of transferred authority to His disciples. "Ye are the branches . . ." He told them (John 15:5). It is a strange use of words. At least eight times in the Old Testament there are messianic prophecies in which Jesus is called "the branch." Zechariah said: "Thus speaketh the Lord of hosts, saying, Behold the man whose name is The BRANCH; and he shall grow up out of his place, and he shall build the temple of the Lord" (Zechariah 6:12).

Most Bible scholars agree this refers to the coming Messiah—Jesus Christ. Jesus was the fulfillment of Zechariah's prophecy. Why then does He confer this title upon His disciples? Is it not that He is preparing, within the next few days, to return to His Father in Heaven? Thus His continuing work shall be carried out by those who not only represent Him but actually go forth with the same power and Spirit that He had when He walked the earth.

Already in John 14, Jesus had told His disciples, "I am in the Father, and the Father in me." Even though He never pretended to be the Vine, He now says that since the Father—who is the Vine—is in Him, then He, too, is the Vine. And because of that He is able to confer upon His followers the identical title earlier conferred upon Him by the prophets. Now He is the Vine, but we are the branches—just as He was the branch while He was on earth.

Are miracles for today? Only if Jesus is for today. For He has not changed—and His Spirit in us is still the same, miracle-working Spirit as when He descended upon Jesus at the Jordan River. By giving us the same Spirit He received at His baptism, He indwells us and empowers us and in and through and by us presents Himself to every generation and every place.

So there you have it. Being filled with His Spirit, we may expect to function in our world as He functioned in the world of the first century. We are the thinking, breathing, feeling, acting Body of Christ in the world. It is His dream which still forms in us, awaiting final fulfillment in our own lives.

The world assumes that each of us is something to be taught or trained—that we are raw material ready to fit someone else's mold. The Bible teaches, however, that each of us has a unique design that can be fulfilled only when we find our place in God's purpose.

The reason there was such power in the early church was they were all in one accord. They were the literal presence of Jesus Christ on earth because they were an integrated, harmonious body—fitly joined together. As long as they remained that way, the same power operated in the church which operated in Jesus Himself. Only when they became divided did the power disintegrate—and only as we come again into unity will His power return in all its fullness.

It is up to each one of us to find God's gift in our lives—and then let the Holy Spirit fulfill His dream in us. As a boy, I dreamed of being a doctor. I yearned to be able to pull my car off the side of the road, rush back to an accident and save someone's life. Then I got to college and discovered there is more to medicine than putting broken arms in splints and administering magical potions which save lives. There is the matter of chemistry, and of mathematics, and of biology. These were my worst subjects, and when I barely squeaked through freshman chemistry and never did learn to use a slide rule, I had to admit I had misinterpreted my gift. Did this mean my dream was shattered? Not at all. Even though I knew I would never make it as a doctor, the desire to help remained. All I needed to do was align my dream with my gift—which, in my case, was that of showing mercy. As each man finds his place in the Body, develops his dream by aligning it with his gift, determined not to be anyone else but to be the person God created him to be—then the Body shall come together and signs and wonders shall once again appear—just as they did in Jesus' day. For it is then that believers, as individuals and in true oneness, will be within the Spirit's control.

Corporations believe it is possible to train a man to fit the needs of the corporation—salesman, management executive, technician, engineer. But if a man does not have the basic spiritual gift which underlies these departments, no amount of training will ever make him happy or effective in that position.

Seminaries often teach young ministers that the pastor of a church needs to be a "well-rounded" person. The minister, we

137

were taught, should not only preach; he should be an administrator, an evangelist, a teacher, a shepherd and give spiritual oversight to the entire Body. In short, the seminary concept is that one man called "the pastor" should do the work that the Apostle Paul said should be handled by at least five men. Not once in my four years of training in a theological seminary was I told to find my place and fulfill my dream as either an apostle, prophet, evangelist, pastor or teacher. It was just assumed I would be all five—despite Paul's admonition to the Ephesians (Ephesians 4:11–16). But just because one has a pastor's heart does not make him a public teacher or an evangelist. Just because one has a burden for lost souls does not mean he is also gifted as a shepherd—or has the insight of a prophet.

Over the years, as I have watched men fail in the ministry, it is often because they have been forced into roles where they were not gifted. The prophet, who had a great gift of preaching and deep spiritual insight, was forced to be a pastor—or an administrator. When he failed in that, and since his preaching was often irritating and pointed, he was forced out of the church. Or perhaps it was a man with a tender, shepherd's heart, who loved his sheep as deeply as he loved his own children. Yet because he was not a prophetic preacher or was a poor evangelist, those in the congregation who wanted to build a bigger, more efficient organization would finally see to it that he was replaced—usually by some kind of human dynamo who shot golf in the high 70s, remembered jokes like Bob Hope and was the darling of the social circle—but knew God only as a distant cousin.

When the church recognizes that God never intended for the spiritual leader to be all things to all people and when the spiritual leaders become secure enough in their gift that they are not threatened by others who can supplement their ministry and succeed in areas where they are weak, then the church will once again grow strong and healthy.

A man is happy and productive only if his work life corresponds with his dream—with the desire of his heart. Self-inventory is absolutely necessary for every Christian, especially those in leadership.

Last year the 10 elders in the Tabernacle Church in Melbourne—

most of whom were in full-time ministry—submitted themselves to a series of vocational tests—the kind given to corporate executives in industry. The purpose was to help us discover our basic, motivational gifts. In short, how to let our dreams come true. After a week of thought and prayer, we withdrew to a small cabin on the beach to spend two days in intense personal evaluation. Each man had jotted down who he really thought he was. Brushing aside "Who do others want me to be?" and "What am I doing now?" each of us focused on such questions as: "What do I really want to do? What is the best contribution I can make to the Body of Christ? What are the real desires of my heart? What is God telling me to do with my life?"

It was an interesting and revealing session. Each man got extremely honest. "You men see me in *this* role," our church administrator said. "But if I were free from all restraints, I would get out of this office and spend all my time as a pastor—ministering to people's needs at the personal level."

Another man confessed he was tired of being thrust into the role of a pastor and counselor. He did it because it was demanded of him. But his real gift was in seeking the Lord in prayer, meditation and through the anguish of the soul, then coming back to the Body as a prophet to speak with strong authority, "This is what God is saying."

I myself confessed I had been playing the role of a pastor for a number of years—first by necessity because there was no one else to do it and later by tradition and habit and because it was expected of me by the people. But deep in my heart I knew my gift was not that of a pastor, even though I shared deep compassion for people. But my basic gift to the local Body was that of a spiritual overseer, fulfilling the apostolic office.

In describing the functions of the "five-fold" ministries Paul outlines in Ephesians 4:11–16, Bob Beckett, one of our pastors, likened it to a human hand. The apostle is the thumb, touching all the other fingers. The prophet is the index finger, jabbing and pointing. The evangelist is the long middle finger, reaching out to the lost. The pastor is the ring finger, calling people into covenant. And the teacher is the little finger, constantly digging for knowledge.

139

A lot of interesting things came to the surface during those few days in the beach cabin. We found we had asked each other to do certain things in order to fill needs rather than because that was God's highest will for the individual. We had not been sensitive to each other's dreams. All of us had assumed responsibilities greater than our capabilities. One of the men finally put his finger on the problem. "The question," he said, "is what are we willing to quit in order to do the things God is asking us to do? The problem is how to differentiate between what I *can* do and what I am *supposed* to do."

In *Up the Organization*, the president of Avis Rent-A-Car tells the story of the fantastic growth of the company. It started with the president saying, "We're going to define our objective." It took six months, but when the dust had settled they had a 23-word objective: "We want to become the fastest growing company, with the highest profit margin, in the business of renting and leasing vehicles without drivers."

To achieve their objective, they had to get rid of everything that didn't fulfill it. Some heads rolled, and a lot of folks got angry, but in the end—after they decided what they were not going to do—they became successful.

Deciding what you are not going to do is equally important with deciding what you are going to do. In fact, you cannot do what you are supposed to do until you stop doing what you are not supposed to.

Producers get life sorted out. They eliminate in order to concentrate. They set up priorities and put on blinders. They learn how to focus. And how to say no.

This is the difference between the achiever and the underachiever. I look around at the people who have achieved and notice all of them have learned the secret of focus. They have learned to say no to the trivial and yes to the important. They have learned to tell the "urgent" to wait until they finish the "important." They have learned to shut out all but the priority issues of life. Like the Apostle Paul, they forget those things which are behind and press on toward the mark of their high calling.

The major difference between a river and a swamp is that the

140

river is going one place while the swamp tries to go everywhere. The river has a goal—an objective. It is determined to reach the sea. The swamp, however, rebels against the discipline of riverbanks and remains a constant underachiever, producing only undesirable things like snakes and mosquitoes—with maybe a few alligators. Although swamps are notorious for bragging about all the territory they cover, they never will experience that glorious satisfaction of achieving one thing—reaching the sea.

Swamps are like a friend of mine who is an expert in nine different areas—from engineering to theology—but can't hold down a single job.

The achiever learns to say no, especially to the good, in order to produce the best. He runs the risk of making people angry, of being called narrow ("What's wrong with breeding a few frogs and snakes?"), but he achieves his goal.

It's not a sin to be a one-talent person. The sin lies in wanting to do 10 things with your one talent and getting so frustrated you wind up achieving nothing at all.

Every so often we catch a glimpse of a man who knows where he is going—a man with a dream who dares invoke the authority of Jesus. In him we see Eden afar off. Through the mist of sin and corruption we say, "That's the way God intends for all of us to be. To live above the fog of perversion and procrastination and achieve, create, conquer."

The world is filled with terribly frustrated people who operate in these areas of illusion, fantasy and deception—never quite able to see the other side of God's purpose for their lives. Often they blame God, charging Him with teasing and taunting them with impossible desires. Yet the wise man soon learns that all dreams do not come from God. Many of them, like my dream of becoming a doctor, are but shadows of our carnal nature, haunting us, taunting us as they never come to pass. It is only when we dare to dig beneath the canopy of desire and tradition to the wellspring of our basic gift that we will discover who we actually are—and find our stream flowing to where we are to be. Until that happens, we continue with our struggles, crying out when our dreams are constantly broken and shattered on the rocks of circumstance which line the inlet to the safe harbor of contentment.

When I started to work on this chapter, I first entitled it, "How to Make Your Dreams Come True." But making dreams come true is the way the world system operates. In the Kingdom, if a dream is of God, and if we allow His principles to govern our lives, the dream will come true. Here, then, is a five-point outline of Kingdom principles designed to let your dreams come true.

Be willing to wait. The kind of dream I am talking about— your deepest hope, the desire of your heart—will not grow up overnight. Such a dream has to materialize, evolve, go through process after process until it is matured. Remember, you may have only one dream for a lifetime. That dream may hit several plateaus along the way, but for most of us there is only one basic dream per person. It is the wise man who is able to focus in and know what that is, to define it exactly.

If you have but one dream to a lifetime, then it's worth waiting a lifetime for it to come to pass. Simeon waited all his life to see the fulfillment of his highest dream—that his eyes would see the Messiah. Doubtless he had been tricked many times before. Surely people had pointed out great leaders and whispered, "That's the Messiah." But there had been no inner witness of the Spirit. So Simeon waited. Like Abraham and Sarah, who waited into old age for the fulfillment of God's promise of a child, hope had nearly faded away. But Simeon held onto his dream. And then one day in the Temple, going about his daily worship as he had for decades, his dream came true.

How much pain we cause ourselves, and others, by trying to fulfill God's best purpose for our lives ahead of time. Young men, young women, starting out into ministry, often feel they need to write a book to give them and their ministry credibility. A great number of these books are written—long before a person has anything to say. A book should grow out of credibility rather than expecting credibility to be established because your name is on a book. Sadly many are unwilling to wait. They hurry their book into production only to wish, years later, they had not said many of the things they earlier put into print. Corrie ten Boom's great books were written after she was 70 years old. Kathryn Kuhlman felt the true story of her life could not be told until after she died. In my own case, even though our church has been on the cutting edge of the Holy Spirit's thrust into this generation, I have resisted all temptations to write that story in detail. That book, like many others snuggling in the womb of creativity, must wait until gestation is complete before it is birthed on paper.

Immature sharing of dreams often brings unneeded heartache. Young Mary, the mother of Jesus, evidenced the wisdom of God when she "kept all these things, and pondered them in her heart" (Luke 2:19). So many of us believe that just because God has whispered something in our ear, it is supposed to be broadcast with our mouth. There is a time to speak—but also a time to keep silent.

There is evidence that Jesus knew as early as age 12 that He was the Messiah—the incarnate Son of God. Yet He willingly submitted Himself to the rule of Joseph and the care of Mary for another 18 years before He made a public announcement of His mission. There were things, necessary things, which needed to come to pass. A great part of His growing in "wisdom and stature, and in favour with God and man" (Luke 2:52) took place in the carpenter's shop. To have stepped out at the age of 12—or at the age of 20—and announced His role as Messiah to the world would have been folly. So He waited. And worked. Until another fullness of time had come and He heard the gentle whisper of the Holy Spirit saying, "Meet me at the Jordan."

Be willing to be misunderstood. Every dreamer is misunderstood by those who do not share his dream. If you have a dream, a vision, if your heart is set on something spiritual and you believe with every fiber of your being that God is one day going to bring it to pass, then you are going to be misunderstood. The Josephs with a far-off look in their eyes are always a threat to men and women living for today alone. Even if you say nothing, the very fact you have a dream will bring persecution.

Martin Luther King's great sermon on the steps of the Lincoln Memorial, "I Have a Dream," stirred more hatred than any sermon

143

ever preached in the United States. He was cutting across the deepest values and traditions of white America. He dreamed of a time when black men would be addressed as "mister" rather than "boy," when black women would be treated with courtesy and respect on city buses, when black children would no longer be called "pickaninnies," when black people were not forced to drink from separate water fountains or use separate restrooms and could sleep in the same motel beds as white people. He dreamed of a day when a black man would be paid the same wages as a white man doing the same work, when children could go to the same public schools as white children, when "for whites only" would be a thing of the dark past. King, like a lot of other visionaries, died for his dream. He died because he was misunderstood.

Visionaries, those with a dream, often have problems with the present. Living out there in the future when the dream, to them, has already come true, often brings them head-on into the bloody facts of the present. Sometimes more practical people have to take them by the hand and lead them as they stagger and bumble through life. Fortunate is the man who has friends around him who at least love him, even though they may never catch his vision or hear the sound of his drummer.

Sometimes, like Joseph, the dreamer is misunderstood because he shares too much too soon. Some pearls should never be scattered across the barnyard—nor shared in the weekly prayer group. If a dream is of God, it will come true even if we keep our mouths shut. In fact, the more close-lipped we are, the better the Holy Spirit is able to work. Only when all the facts have come into place does a man like Jesus rise in the synagogue and say, "The Spirit of the Lord is upon me." Only then does a group of church leaders, fasting and praying and waiting before the Lord, finally lay hands on two men—Barnabas and Paul—and send them forth on the earth's first missionary journey of the early church.

To a real degree the ability to wait is directly involved with the amount of misunderstanding you generate. The classic example is the Apostle Paul. Converted on the road to Damascus—and blinded at the same time—he went immediately into the city where he waited three days in the house of Judas before he received his sight and was filled with the Holy Spirit. However, impatient, over-zealous, and filled with enthusiasm, he straightway went into the synagogues of the city and began preaching that Jesus was the Son of God. It almost cost him his life. In just a few days, when the other believers in the city discovered a plot on his life, they lowered him over the city wall in a basket so he could escape into the desert of Arabia. This segment of his life ends with Acts 9:25.

According to Paul's letter to the Galatians, he remained in the desert for three years—in the seminary of the Holy Spirit. When the story resumes in Acts 9:26, it is three years later. But Paul's nature is the same. Roaring into Jerusalem, he joins the local church and immediately begins to preach—as he did in Damascus. Argumentative in nature, he sought out Jews and Greeks to debate. After only two weeks the entire city was in a turmoil and despite Barnabas' intercession the church could take no more of Paul's immature visionary nature. Again, hearing of a plot to kill him, the Christians rushed him out of the city to the coastal town of Caesarea and put him on a ship for his hometown of Tarsus in Asia Minor. The very day he was kicked out of the church, a revival broke forth. "Then had the churches rest throughout all Judaea and Galilee and Samaria, and were edified; and walking in the fear of the Lord, and in the comfort of the Holy Ghost, were multiplied" (Acts 9:31).

Five years passed and finally the church at Jerusalem sent Barnabas as an apostle to minister to a number of new Greek believers at Antioch. Shortly after he arrived, he departed for Tarsus to find Saul and to ask him to minister with him in Antioch. For two years—from 42 A.D. until 44 A.D.—Saul worked quietly in Antioch, perhaps making tents as he ministered with the other men in leadership position. Finally one day, as five of the leaders were fasting and praying, the Holy Spirit spoke and said, "It's time to send Saul into public ministry" (Acts 13:1–3). Thus began the early church's first missionary journey—10 years after Saul's conversion on the road to Damascus. Interestingly, the change that had taken place in Saul's life was immediately recognized in a change in his name. From that time on, he was no longer called Saul, but Paul.

Paul's dream had not diminished over that 10-year period. If anything, it had enlarged. Neither had his enthusiasm waned. But his maturity was reflected in his ability to wait, patiently, for God to speak—rather than rushing out and trying to convert the world in one giant crusade.

Dreamers are misunderstood because very few people, even those close to them, understand what God is saying. The best you can expect is they will love you, even though they will not understand.

Be willing to work. While dreams come true for cripples as well as those whole in body, all are commanded to work until that dream is fulfilled.

Paul is blunt in his word to the lazy Christians at Thessalonica who seemed to think all they had to do was sit around and wait for manna to fall from heaven—or perhaps let the church feed them.

For even when we were with you, this we commanded you, that if any would not work, neither should he eat. For we hear that there are some which walk among you disorderly, working not at all, but are busybodies. Now them that are such we command and exhort by our Lord Jesus Christ, that with quietness they work, and eat their own bread (2 Thessalonians 3:10–12).

The man who works with his hands, who labors with the sweat of his brow, opens up avenues for God to speak to him at the same time—avenues never opened to the lazy Christian. God never speaks to lazy people. A survey through the Bible indicates that God always called busy men when He had a dream to fulfill.

"You, Abram. You've been busy for 75 years tending the flocks of old Terah; I have a dream for you to fulfill . . ."

"You, Moses, busy for these last 40 years herding sheep and goats for Jethro, I have a dream for you to fulfill . . ."

"You, Gideon, over there behind the winepress working with the grapes, I have a dream for you to fulfill . . ."

"You, beautiful Ruth, busy gleaning the fields of Boaz, I have a dream for you to fulfill . . ."

"You, young Samuel, busy cleaning out the Temple at Shiloh and making sure the lamps are always burning at the altar, I have a dream for you to fulfill . . ."

"You, Amos, busy harvesting figs down in Judah, I have a dream for you to fulfill up in Israel . . ."

"You, Jesus, there in the carpenter's shop, it is time to lay aside your apron and hammer. I have a dream for you to fulfill . . ."

God seldom speaks to people to go off on long retreats and sit under trees with their mouths open, waiting for some especially tasty word to fall in. What He does is let you sit there until you get exceedingly hungry and for sheer preservation are forced to go to work with your hands. Then, in the process of hammering nails, digging fence-post holes in the swamp, driving a taxi or working behind a cash register, He calls you by name. At that time He may tell you to quit work but only because He has a far greater task for you to do. He never calls men to idleness.

If you want your dreams to come true, get to work. Do things with your hands. Sweat with your brow. Get to work 10 minutes early and work 15 minutes past quitting time—without asking for overtime. Walk the second mile for your boss. Give him your cloak when he demands your coat. Turn the other cheek when he slaps you with his insensitivity to your personal needs. Dream up new methods. Innovate. Improve the business. Go to school in your spare time. Come in and work when no one else knows you are working. Whatever your hand finds to do, do it with all your might.

And your dreams will come true. Not because you've worked and brought them into being, but because God honors the worker and will bless you accordingly.

Dreams come true when a man does an honest day's work for a full day's pay. Just because a man has a doctor's degree in theology does not mean he is disqualified from laying bricks or pumping septic tanks. Sometimes that's the best therapy in the world.

Recently a well educated man arrived in our community saying he needed work. We discovered he had taught history on a graduate level in a large university but had been fired when a student accused him of immorality. Out of that he had come to know the Lord, even though he had lost his wife and family in the process. Now he was in Melbourne, asking us to help him.

"What is your biggest need?" I asked him.

"Money," he said a bit embarrassed. "I may go to jail if I cannot pay off some of my debts."

"Fine," I said, "I know how you can get money. Lots of it. I have a friend who owns a septic tank service. He needs someone to drive the 'honey truck' and handle the pumping. At the end of the week he pays you money."

The professor was insulted and soon moved on to another town. Somehow he had never related the fact that work and money go together. Perhaps he thought it just flowed automatically from the administration building, or he had been taught in his early days as a Christian that to trust in God meant to open your Bible each morning and there would be a 20 dollar bill tucked neatly into Romans. Fortunately that is not so. We live in a very practical world. God expects us to do practical things. If Paul, the Pharisee of the Pharisees and a member of the Sanhedrin with a doctorate of theology, could sit on the curb with his bare feet smelling of camel dung and sew tents for a living—in order to carry on his ministry—then it should not be below any of us, especially those of us with dreams yet to be fulfilled, to perform the menial if that's what it takes.

Be willing for God to twist you until you are the right shape to contain your dream. God cannot put round dreams into square containers. So He twists. Molds. Reshapes until we are prepared to hold all He has for us.

If Jesus Christ is Lord, then He can do with you what He chooses. To bring you to that place where the dream He has placed within your heart can come to pass, He often has to do a great deal of reshaping. That sometimes causes pain, humiliation, even death. Sometimes it means we are bruised or scratched. We can choose to blame Satan when we undergo tough times if we want, but if our dream is legitimate—if it comes from God—then it is not the devil who is twisting our life but the Holy Spirit. God allows these things to come into your life for the purpose of making

148

you a fit container for His dream. Plastic surgery is often painful, especially when it is done in public, but at the same time it is necessary if we are to reflect God's grace.

Last Wednesday morning, before I sat down at the typewriter to finish this chapter, the telephone rang. It was the wife of a former evangelist. We had known the family for several years, but things had not gone well in his family. He and his wife had divorced, and shortly afterwards he married again. He had dropped out of all church activity and gone into a lucrative business selling insurance to churches. Occasionally I would question him about his dream, but he would always shrug and say, "Later, after things calm down and I get out of debt." But I was unable to figure out how he could get out of debt as long as he was buying a new Mercedes every year and eating at the most expensive restaurants in town. I tried to be kind, but I knew I was speaking truth when I told him, "If you don't begin to cooperate with the purposes and principles of God, then God, who has a claim on your life, is going to twist you and bend you against your will until you do cooperate. You have no choice but to do His will or be broken as you beat yourself against that will."

That, you see, is the nature of God, the nature of His love. He loves us so much He will do anything to shape us into the image of His Son, Jesus Christ.

Then this morning his wife called.

"We're in trouble," she said simply, her voice quivering.

"I'm listening," I replied.

"Tom's son was involved in an accident last night. Two people were killed. One of them was a baby."

She went ahead to blurt out the details. Tom's 17-year-old son by his previous marriage, who was visiting with them for the weekend, had stopped by a bar after a teen-age dance. The bartender had refused to serve him since he was underage. Angry and embarrassed in front of his friend, he stormed out of the bar, got in his father's new Mercedes and roared out of the parking lot straight into the path of a small car carrying a young couple just returning from the hospital with their newborn baby. The mother and child had been killed instantly. The father was critically injured. Both cars were demolished. The son, frightened and alone, had fled the accident on foot and was later picked up by the police and was in jail.

"I know God is working in his life," the stepmother said. Then she paused, choking on tears, "and in ours, too."

The love of God does not let us go. When Samuel told Israel, "For the Lord will not forsake his people . . ." he also added, "But if ye shall still do wickedly, ye shall be consumed " (1 Samuel 12:22, 25). Sometimes God's people might wish God would forsake them, leave them alone. But once the commitment has been made, God never breaks His contract. He is always there, the mighty Hound of Heaven, tracking us down and arranging or allowing circumstances to take place which are designed to conform us to the image of His Son Jesus.

The Bible is filled with stories of men running from God. Samson. Balaam. King Saul. David. Jonah. Elijah. My friend, the former evangelist, was in good company. The Hound of Heaven was still nipping at his heels. But the man of God on the run from God is the most miserable of all people. And so, in the midst of crisis, my friend came the next day to say, with the Apostle Paul, "I can no longer fight God." He has a long way to go, but now with his spirit softened, he, his wife and his son are prepared soil for the seeds of the Kingdom to take root and grow. Just this morning he called, saying even though his son was out of jail, he was still committed to turn his back on the systems of the world and return to the true God.

Was God in all that? Did God design a tragic automobile accident where innocent people were killed, and a lonely boy was battered for life? Such questions cannot be answered, except with other questions. Are the sins of the fathers visited upon the children? Is God still in control of the world? Can it be possible that life on this earth is relatively inconsequential when compared with all that is before us in eternity? Can God take even a tragedy like this and use it for His glory? Is it possible that dreams have not been dashed into irreparable damage but rather are indeed being worked out despite those involved?

The answer to these questions, of course, depends on the size and power of God rather than our ability to understand Him. Thus it is not fair to ask if God was responsible for the tragedy until you have the answers to the other questions. For our dreams are too small. It is only God's dream, in the long run, which counts.

Finally: *Be willing for that dream to come to pass through somebody else.* Let's return to old Simeon, wandering around the Temple, holding onto his dream. There is no way Simeon could have known the Messiah was going to come in the form of a tiny baby. No doubt like all others he pictured the Messiah as another Maccabean deliverer, riding into Jerusalem on a white horse with flashing sword to deliver the Jews from the hated Roman tyrants. So he had practiced his little speech for years and imagined how he would fall on his knees before that magnificent specimen of manhood who like Jupiter would spring in full maturity from the heart of God. But Simeon's thoughts were not God's thoughts, and one day in the Temple the Holy Spirit whispered to Simeon, "There! See over there! See that father talking to the priest? See that young mother holding the little baby right behind them? That little child is the Messiah of the House of Israel, the light to lighten the Gentiles, the Holy One of Israel. There He is. Take Him in your arms and bless Him. Your dream has come true."

So it is with us. So often we have our hearts set on one thing, and God shows us something else. But what He shows us is so much better than what we thought we wanted; it brings nothing but joy.

David thought his dream of the magnificent Temple would come true through him. But God had another plan. And the dream came to pass through David's son, Solomon.

Moses dreamed of a promised land and led his people to the mountain where they could look across and see the green valley of Jericho in the distance. But it was up to Joshua, who was like a son to old Moses, to lead the people into Canaan.

Paul dreamed of Spain—and wound up in a Roman prison.

John Hus dreamed of a time when the common people could drink of the cup of Jesus' blood. But he wound up at the executioner's block. Latimer and Ridley dreamed of a time when the Bible would be available to all people—and were tied to stakes and set

151

afire. Martin King dreamed of a society without prejudice and was killed by an assassin's bullet. But dreams live beyond men, for the dreams coming from the heart of God are always bigger than the dreamers—and bigger than those who try to stop them.

In Hebrews 11, Paul lists the heroes of the faith. Then he closes out the chapter with a list of other men who never did see their dreams come true. They were tortured, mocked, imprisoned, stoned, sawn asunder, slain with the sword, wandered about in skins, were destitute, afflicted, and tormented. It is not the same picture often presented to us by mail-order evangelists who tell us if we send them money in an envelope, our dreams will come true. At the end of the chapter, Paul reminds us that they "received not the promise." Faith teachers often say that all the promises of God are for us. But we must remember the promises are always bigger than our comprehension. In this case, Paul says, "God having provided some better thing for us, that they without us should not be made perfect" (Hebrews 11:40).

We are the continuing fulfillment of their dream—just as we are the continuing fulfillment of Jesus' dream. So the question remains for all of us: Can we release even our dreams to God, to let them come to pass in His time and His way—not ours?

It's a venture we shouldn't miss.

IX

Our Times in God's Hands

I was sitting in the back of the large auditorium with some of the other conference speakers, enjoying the opening session. More than a thousand youth leaders had gathered at the beautiful 4-H retreat center at Rock Eagle, Georgia, for a three-day conference sponsored by the Tennessee-Georgia Christian Camps I was to teach a daily seminar and then speak to the large assembly on Saturday. However, like the other speakers on the program, I wanted to attend all the sessions to catch the "mood" of the conference as it progressed.

Rock Eagle is about an hour's drive from Atlanta and about the same distance from Macon. The camp is nestled in the heavily wooded red hills of Georgia, very quiet, very secluded. People had come from all over the Southeast for the conference and were staying in the various cabins scattered over the large retreat grounds.

We had arrived only a few hours earlier on that Thursday. In fact, some of the people were still in their cabins unpacking as the first session began in the auditorium. Larry Tomczak, a Roman Catholic lay-evangelist who is pastor of a large interdenominational youth-oriented group in Washington, D.C., was the opening night speaker. Larry is a special friend and, seated in the far back of the auditorium with the other speakers, I looked forward to his message for the evening.

But Larry was too excited to get right into his message. He had some personal stories he wanted to tell first. His wife was expecting their first child—due in a couple of weeks—and he was pretty wound up about the miracle of childbirth. I chuckled inwardly as he talked excitedly about the wonderful thing that was about to happen. After all, when you've gone through five such events, although the thrill remains, the excitement is not quite so intense.

But Larry's excitement was at the pinnacle, and he seemed determined to give the audience a blow-by-blow description of everything that had happened to them since the moment of conception, eight and a half months before. I was impressed with his enthusiasm over becoming a father but a little bored with his long discourse. After all, after you've had five of your own . . .

But there was no way to tone down his passion and eloquence of description. He shared what happened when his wife first discovered she was pregnant—his feelings and hers.

"I held her for a long time," he said. "Not only had she created new life, but I was responsible. My wife and I had created a new life which was already alive in her body—waiting to be born."

Larry was convinced the baby was a boy. So convinced he immediately picked out a name and began ministering to the baby. "Every night before bedtime, my wife would lie on the bed, and I would lay my hands on her stomach and minister to the child, speak to him, comfort him, remind him that he was a child of God, impart my love to him as his father."

Now that's interesting, I thought, sitting up a bit as I took notice. Larry said he had been doing this from the very first night they discovered his wife was pregnant. He would speak directly to the child, preparing him for the great event of birth, telling him not to be afraid, that there were some folks waiting for him who loved him and were eager to greet him when he arrived. Not only that, but he was going to be born into a much larger family of brothers and sisters in the Washington area, all of whom were eagerly awaiting his arrival.

"If John the Baptist could be filled with the Holy Spirit in his mother's womb," Larry said, "then why not my son?" So he had been praying that his son would be baptized in the Holy Spirit even before he was born. Now it was almost time for the baby to arrive. I began to understand why Larry was so excited.

Just as he was finishing his story and getting into his message for the evening, I felt a gentle tap on my shoulder. Looking back, I saw a man leaning over the back row and motioning for me to slip out and join him in the vestibule of the auditorium. The back rows were not crowded so I was able to leave without causing a disturbance. Once in the vestibule, the man said, "Could you come with me? A friend of yours, Bo Reed, sent me over from our cabin. We have an emergency going on and need your help."

Bo, a CPA from Boca Raton, Florida, has been helping me with my accounting problems for several years. I knew he and his wife, Carol, were staying in a cabin with a young couple from Macon, Georgia. I also knew he would not call me out of a meeting unless it was important, so I went with the man out into the darkness and down a long path to a lighted cabin.

Bo and Carol met me at the door of the cabin and explained the situation. The young wife from Macon was about three months pregnant and had begun to hemorrhage. They didn't know anyone else at the conference to call but me. Could I help?

"It sounds like she needs a doctor, not a writer," I said.

"I know," Bo said, putting his hand on my shoulder. "But somehow the Lord kept telling me I should call you first."

"Where is she?" I asked.

"She's in the bedroom with her husband. It's their first child, and he's frantic. She's been bleeding for more than an hour and is in a lot of pain. It's a pretty tense situation right now."

I slipped into the cabin, down the hall to the bedroom and stood in the door. The young wife was stretched out on a cot, writhing in pain. Her face contorted, her body twisting with intense cramps. Her husband was pacing the floor, dropping to his knees beside her, then up to the wash basin to get a cold cloth for her head. He looked at me, and there was deep anguish on his face.

"We're more than an hour away from her doctor in Macon,"

155

he said. "I don't know whether to move her or what. We need help."

I glanced at Bo. "Ask everyone to leave the bedroom. Including her husband. I want to be alone with her for a few moments."

I closed the door behind them and knelt beside the young woman on the bed. I had no idea what I was going to do, but I knew the intensity of all those people in and out of the room was not helping things. As I knelt, I remembered what Larry had been talking about just moments before in the auditorium. At the time I wondered why he was going into such great detail. Now I realized it was far more than coincidence. God was at work.

Kneeling beside the girl, aware she was in danger of a miscarriage, I put my hand on her stomach. It was hard and taut. I could feel the muscles rippling beneath her dress as they undulated back and forth in cramps. She was moaning, her body twisting and convulsing.

"Just relax," I said softly, as she looked down at me with eyes wide with fear. "God is in control here."

Fortunately she knew who I was and gave a little sideways smile. "I'm not going to talk to you," I said gently. "But you can listen if you want. I'm going to talk to this little life in your tummy. I'm going to minister to this baby who is trying to kick his way free."

She nodded and smiled again, then let out a scream of pain as her stomach once again convulsed in an excruciating cramp.

It seemed so natural. Having heard Larry helped; but what I was doing seemed the most natural thing in the world. As an adult I was taking authority over an unruly child. And even though I knew the baby could not hear me—or even if it could it could not understand—nevertheless I realized I was setting some spiritual principles in motion which would cause the child to obey. The fear and anxiety which had filled the room earlier had only caused the child to be more frightened. Now I was trusting that the spirit of love and power and a sound mind would cast out that fear, and it would be replaced with a spirit of authority and submission.

"Little baby . . ." It sounded so strange. Maybe I should talk a little louder. I raised my voice. "Little baby, you don't know me. In fact, you don't know anyone. That's your problem. You're lost and lonely and afraid. But I've been sent here by your Creator to tell you that you are a child of God. You have been created by God. But you've not met Him because you're all closed up in there. But I want to tell you about Him. He's a loving Father. He's taking care of you. He put you there, and He wants you to stop all that fussing and kicking and rebelling. You don't need to be afraid. You don't need to try to kick your way out of that pocket you're in. Your life is in the hands of the heavenly Father. If He wants to come get you and take you home, that's His business. If He wants you to stay inside your mother and grow, that's His business, too. You don't have to worry about it. Now, in the name of God's Son, Jesus, I tell you to lie down and be quiet. You've got everything you need in there. Just relax and be quiet; God is in control."

As I was going through this little procedure, I kept my hands on the young woman's stomach, resting gently, not moving. Beneath my fingers I could actually feel her stomach begin to relax; the swelling went down, the tight muscles loosened. She had her knees pulled up, but as I ministered to her baby, she straightened out on the bed. The moaning and screaming had stopped. When I finished speaking, I looked up at her. Her head was back on the pillow. She was asleep.

I breathed a quick *thank You* to my Father and tiptoed out into the hall where her husband and his little group of friends were standing in an anxious huddle. I spoke to the young man.

"She's asleep. Relaxed. The cramping has stopped. I suggest you find a telephone and call your obstetrician in Macon and tell him what has happened. I am sure he is going to ask you to bring her to the hospital so she can be examined. But everything is all right. She and the child are in God's hands."

I returned to the auditorium in time to catch the last of Larry's message. The next morning I learned the rest of the story. The doctor had asked the husband to bring her to the hospital in Macon. They had put her in the back seat of the car so she could stretch out. She had gone back to sleep and sometime during that ride, before they reached the hospital, she miscarried. But she slept all

157

the way through the ordeal. The Lord, who had put the child in her body, had taken the child for reasons unknown this side of Glory. But He did it with decency, order and peace.

As I reflected on the entire event, I became aware once again of the sovereignty of God. Our times are indeed, as David said, "in His hands." It is God who gives life and God who takes it away. There is no reason for us to walk through life with a chip on our shoulder or our fists balled up, anticipating a fight. People who go through life like that always meet someone ready to take on their challenge. The Romans used to say, *Si vis pacem, para bellum.* (If you wish peace, prepare for war.) This is still the theme of our Department of Defense. But in the Kingdom of God the very opposite is true. He who is servant is leader, he who is last is first, he who ministers peace is the strongest warrior. As God's children we can walk through this world unafraid, for our times are in His hands. He is in sovereign control of our lives and of this universe.

We often forget that. We forget it when we are tense, anxious, when the money runs out, when our job is terminated, when the doctor says we have cancer, when the little baby inside begins to try to get out. We forget that God is in control of His world— and especially of His children.

There is an interesting story in Mark 4 which illustrates this. All day Jesus had been teaching along the shore of the Sea of Galilee. When evening came, He asked His disciples, most of whom were fishermen and had their own boats, to take Him to the other side of the big lake. But His request was more than a suggestion; it was a positive affirmation. "Let us pass over unto the other side" (Mark 4:35).

Since all the disciples could not get in the one boat, they took several other smaller boats also. Jesus, who was physically tired, settled down in the stern of the boat, put His head on a pillow and went to sleep. As still happens on the Galilee, a great storm arose without any warning and suddenly the tiny ships were in danger of being capsized. Water was pouring in over the gunwales. The disciples were bailing, but it looked like the ships were going down. Seeing Jesus still asleep in the midst of this horrible storm, one of the men cried out: "Master, carest thou not that we perish?" It was a simple, human cry. "Master, do something!"

Jesus woke up. Seeing the fear on the faces of the disciples, He spoke to the sea: "Peace, be still." Immediately the wind ceased to blow, the huge waves subsided, and the storm was over.

Then turning to His followers, Jesus rebuked them. "Why all this fear? Have you no faith?"

That remark used to bother me, for it seemed to be an unjust rebuke. Who wouldn't be afraid in a situation like that? But you cannot understand Mark unless you remember Mark. Before they embarked, Jesus had affirmed: "We're going to the other side."

Faith is believing God will do what He says, regardless of the height of the waves. Fear causes us to look at the circumstances. Faith causes us to look at God. It is the gift which enables us to go to sleep in the middle of a storm, knowing God has promised we will cross over—or go to sleep in the middle of a miscarriage, knowing God is in total control.

As the ongoing ministry of Jesus, not only do we have faith to believe God's word will bring us through, but we have the authority to speak to the elements—just as Jesus did—if they get in the way of God's intent and purpose.

Spiritual authority is one of the attributes which accompanies salvation and the Spirit-controlled life, yet it is so seldom used. How vividly I remember the reply Corrie ten Boom gave when asked about a certain missionary family who were under great attack on the mission field, harassed by circumstances, defeated by sickness, plagued by evil spirits. The fabled old Dutch woman shook her head sadly. "They have given all, but they have not taken all."

How desperately we need to take the authority God has given us and defeat the enemies which surround us. The authority to lay hands on the tummy of a young woman and speak to that life inside, kicking its heels and rebelling, and say, "In the name of Jesus, little baby, lie down and relax."

Shortly after I had been baptized in the Holy Spirit, I received a call from the principal of the high school in the community where we lived, asking me to preach the sermon to the graduating

159

class at baccalaureate. The high school had never had a baccalaureate service before, but since several of the graduating seniors attended our little church, they put pressure on the school administration who agreed. It was to be a big affair in the football stadium the first Sunday night in June.

I gave little thought to it for we were having our own problems in the church about that time. We lived in a transient community and a number of our people were either associated with the nearby space center or stationed at Patrick Air Force Base. As a result, people were constantly moving in and out of the community—more out than in. Our church had grown even smaller than the original 40 families we began with a year before and now my open declaration that I had been "baptized in the Holy Spirit" had everyone on edge, wondering what was going to happen next. They did take some comfort, however, that I had been asked to deliver the first baccalaureate sermon at the big high school and, realizing that 80 percent of the young people in the high school were "unchurched," had been praying for me.

Three days before the scheduled Sunday evening service in the football stadium, the east coast of Florida was buffeted by a preseason hurricane which came roaring through the Caribbean and up the Atlantic seacoast until it reached the city of Melbourne. Mysteriously it remained stationary, about 10 miles off the coast, dumping tons of water on our city. It rained torrents for 48 hours straight. Sunday morning the high school principal called my house.

"We have almost three inches of water on the grass turf at the stadium," he said. "If it doesn't stop raining by four o'clock this afternoon, we're calling off the baccalaureate service."

I went to church that morning in an anxious mood. Ordinarily I'm not too eager to speak at community functions, but this was different. For the first time in my life, I felt I had something to share with the people. I had met a God of miracles, and I was eager to introduce Him to the students and their parents. But I couldn't do a thing unless the rain stopped. With the eye of the hurricane directly off the coast, however, there was no way. Even if the hurricane began to move, it would not be far enough away by evening for the rain to cease.

That afternoon I called five or six of the men in the church and asked them to meet me at the Tabernacle at 3 P.M. to pray. They sensed my urgency and agreed to be there. We arrived in the pouring rain and dashed to the shelter of the building. We stood in a circle in the side of our little meeting room and held hands. The rain was falling so hard we could scarcely make ourselves heard. One by one the men prayed.

"Lord, you control the weather. Please make it stop raining."

"Lord, you opened the Red Sea; now part the clouds so we can have the service tonight."

"Lord, we believe you ordained Jamie to speak tonight, but he can't do it in the rain. Isn't there something you can do about it?"

"Lord, you created the sun and the rain, and we sure need the sun right now rather than the rain."

They were all good, honest, sincere prayers. But nothing happened. In fact, I don't think we really expected anything to happen. We were just praying because we didn't know what else to do.

Then it was my time to pray. But when I opened my mouth, instead of the usual Baptist "sentence prayer," I heard myself saying something that was so ridiculous I was shocked. But the words just poured forth. I was shouting.

"IN THE MIGHTY NAME OF JESUS, I COMMAND YOU CLOUDS TO GO AWAY! I COMMAND YOU RAIN TO STOP FALLING! I REBUKE YOU, EVIL HURRICANE, AND COMMAND YOU TO DEPART! OPEN, CLOUDS, AND LET THE SUN SHINE THROUGH!"

My word! Had that come out of me? I had never spoken like that before. I looked around at the other men, still standing in our circle holding hands. They were all staring at me—and I could understand why. None of us, including me, seemed to want to hang around any longer. I choked out, "Let's go home." We all picked up our rain coats and umbrellas and headed for the door.

But instead of walking out into the rain, we walked out into brilliant sunshine. Water was everywhere. The streets were flooded up over the curbs and sidewalks. Water was dripping from the trees and plants. But overhead the sky was blue and the summer sun was shining through, reflecting off the water below

"Hallelujah!" one of the men shouted. Then, catching himself, he blushed. We dashed to our cars, but I knew something had happened in that room that would not only change my life forever, but change the lives of those men who were with me.

That night I preached the baccalaureate sermon to a group of kids who marched out on the field in caps and gowns, barefooted. All around us we could see the rain falling in sheets. But the football stadium was under clear skies. The Methodist pastor who gave the invocation asked me before I marched out on the field if I wasn't going to take my umbrella in case it rained. I'm sure he didn't understand my grin when I said, "Not after what I've just been through."

I had never preached with such power. And authority. And when I shared about the reality of a miracle-working God, I knew I was speaking from personal experience—not from someone else's testimony. By the time we were back at the car after the service, it had started to rain again—and continued to rain for another 24 hours before the hurricane moved out to sea and dissipated.

The idea that God is speaking today—and that we are able to hear Him—is foreign to most of us. People who "hear voices" are considered strange. If you "act on that voice," you are considered psychotic. Yet, when we stop and consider that God has not just set certain laws in motion by which the universe is run and then stepped back out of the way but still intervenes in the affairs of men through His Son Jesus Christ, and that we are the Body of Christ here on earth—well, how else will God speak unless it is through one of us?

Recently I was one of the invited speakers at a convention of Christian businessmen in a northern city. Several thousand people were in attendance, filling the ballroom for three days at the beautiful Hilton Hotel. The singing was beautiful, many of the messages were inspired and there seemed to be some genuine spiritual activity taking place as people committed themselves to the Lord, and some were even healed.

However, as is sometimes the case, some of the leaders got caught up in the spiritual excitement and began to think they were in control. I first noticed it at the Saturday morning meeting. I had spoken Friday night and the meeting had been good. Solid. But the next morning, as I was sitting on the platform with the other speakers and a number of Christian leaders, I sensed things were becoming commercial. It started with a series of marketing announcements in the worship service—selling books (including some of mine), tapes and records. I have always been uncomfortable when this happens. It is one thing to make the books and tapes available for those who want to purchase them but another thing to hawk them from the platform as one might sell snake oil from the tailgate of a covered wagon. Later in the meeting the same commercial spirit was exhibited when the platform leader launched into a long, emotional appeal on the sad state of finances in the organization. This was followed by an offering in which he asked people to pledge money on a monthly basis. "Who will give $1,000 per month? Who will give $500? Who will give $100 per month to keep this great organization alive?" People stood, to the applause of others, and waved their checkbooks to indicate the amount of their pledge. I was appalled. And saddened.

Then the song leader, a short man with a big voice, began playing the role of religious cheerleader. Employing a number of hackneyed gimmicks, including some "Jesus cheers," he tried to whip the people into an emotional frenzy. There is a place for joyful applause, dancing in the Spirit, even shouting. But such activity must be inspired, fueled and directed by the Holy Spirit—not by some grasshopper leading a cheering section.

I was sickened, but I held my peace. It did not seem appropriate for an invited guest, one sitting on the platform at that, to interrupt the meeting and bring correction. Besides, several of those in charge of the meeting served on the board of one of the publishing companies which was paying part of my salary. So, to a degree, not only was I a guest but an employee as well.

During one of the moments while the song leader was catching his breath between choruses, there was a sudden interruption in the meeting. From the back of the room came an utterance in tongues. The room grew silent as the man spoke, strong, forcefully, in an unknown tongue. I have never given a public utterance in tongues, and only on rare occasions have I felt I had an interpretation for such an utterance. But this time, as the man continued speaking, I began receiving the interpretation. It was as clear as

163

any word I have ever received. I could almost hear what God was telling me to say when the utterance was completed. I was terrified, and knew I could not speak what I was hearing:

"I am appalled by what is going on in this place in my name. You have quenched my Holy Spirit who wants to lead you into holy places of worship. You are making a mockery out of praise . . . you have turned my house of prayer into a den of thieves . . . your sounds come before me as a stench in my nostrils. Be still, and I will move sovereignly among you . . ."

There was more. It was coming so fast I could scarcely remember it. I knew it was God's word for that group at that time. The man speaking in tongues stopped. Again there was a moment of silence. I knew I should speak out. But I was afraid. I was an invited guest. I was sitting on the platform surrounded by great men of God. Who was I, a newcomer, to inject such a harsh message of condemnation? I stood silently, my head bowed, hoping someone else would give the interpretation but knowing no one else would; for God had given it to me. Alone.

The silence lasted only a moment. The song leader, having caught his breath, seemed offended that anyone—including God—would interrupt his method of leadership. "How about another chorus?" he beamed. And he was off and running, thumping the pulpit and clapping his hands in time to the music.

Inwardly I was burning with relief—and shame. When we finally sat down, I reached under my chair to adjust some papers when the man next to me, an older minister from another state whom I had met only that morning, leaned over and whispered in my ear.

"You had the interpretation for that utterance in tongues. Why didn't you speak it out?"

I could hardly straighten up. It felt like someone had kicked me in the pit of my stomach and driven all the air out of me. I knew my face had turned crimson. I looked up and tried to speak, but nothing came out. "I-I-I . . ."

He shook his head and said with finality, "You should always be obedient when God tells you to do something. We all needed to hear His word at that moment."

I remember very little about the rest of that meeting. Later in my hotel room I sat with several friends and explained what had happened. They, too, had felt God was trying to interrupt the soulish activity to bring His order—but none of them had received the direct word. Only I. And I had been too scared to speak. However, as I prayed in my room with my friends, I made a fresh commitment to God. From that time on, if God told me to say something, I would do it. Better to be criticized by man than to disappoint God.

God is seeking men and women willing to be His voice, His hands, containers for His power, dispensers of His love. He is waiting for men and women to step forward saying, "Our times are in your hands—we trust you with our lives."

X

The Jonah Complex

I don't even remember what we were arguing about. It all seems so nonsensical now—but then it must have been a pretty big thing. It probably centered around the fact I pay more attention to other people than I do to her.

That particular day the children were at school and the house had been quiet most of the morning. I had been in my studio working and had emerged for lunch. While Jackie was putting the last items on the table, I made a quick phone call to my secretary to see if anything had come up during the morning which needed attention. When I hung up, Jackie commented something to the effect that it would have been nice had she been the first person I spoke to when I appeared from my study. I should have admitted I was preoccupied, apologized and given her a big hug—which was all she really wanted. Instead, I made some snide remark about the difficulties of moving into spiritual maturity. And suddenly we were in the middle of a fight.

I don't react very well when I am hungry—or preoccupied. And that day I was both. Before I knew it, I was angry. The argument moved, as most marital arguments do, from the original point of contention to numerous other subjects—including some of my past mistakes. Lunch was forgotten as we stalked each other around

167

the kitchen, each trying to prove our point. Frustrated, I finally picked up a heavy salt shaker and, before I could think, smashed it against the wall above the breakfast table.

The salt shaker disintegrated into a thousand slivers of pottery, which, mixed with the salt, went everywhere—especially over the sandwiches and into soup already on the table. Fortunately, the beautiful yellow and white wallpaper was not cut, but there was a large, squishy indentation in the gypsum wallboard behind it— a scar which remains to this day.

As usual, Jackie decided that was a good time to leave the room. I got the whisk broom and a thin piece of cardboard and went to work, on my knees, cleaning up the mess. That is an ideal position in which to repent. Which I did. When it was all over and the kitchen was back to normal—minus one rosebud salt shaker from Jackie's favorite "Desert Rose" pattern and plus one squishy indentation in the wall over the breakfast table—I went to find my wife and apologize. She was upstairs, stretched out on the bed, reading her Bible.

"We both needed to skip lunch anyway," she said, after I apologized for my behavior and for showering our food with tiny slivers of pottery.

We sat and talked for a long time. I talked about my explosive nature, which was not nearly as bad as it used to be, but still an insult to me and others around me. She talked about her insecurities and petty jealousies and why she was always demanding from me more than was reasonable for me to give. We traced our actions back to various times in our past when we had been wounded. Then we prayed together and spent a little time making up. Forty-five minutes later, when all the emotions had passed, Jackie rather nonchalantly said, "Have you ever read the last chapter of Jonah?"

I lay back on the bed, thinking that arguments weren't so bad if they all wound up this way. I gradually realized she was talking to me, and I asked her to repeat it.

"While you were down there cleaning up your mess, I came up here, opened the Bible and was reading the Book of Jonah. Have you ever read the last chapter?"

168

I thought. Jonah? Well, it had been a long time since I had read the first chapters. Even then, I had to admit I had stopped at the whale.

"I think you ought to read the entire book," Jackie said. "I think it will reveal some things about your anger—and your inability to control it."

I felt myself growing tense again. Why did she have to spoil such a peaceful moment with preaching? Then I recalled our conversation, how we had been so honest with each other regarding our frailties and flaws. Why shouldn't I listen to her? After all, I expected her to listen to me. So I promised her that before the day was over I would sit down and read the entire Book of Jonah—all two and one-half pages of it.

After dinner that night and after the children had gone to town for a football game, Jackie and I were alone again. She was sitting at the dining room table with her checkbook and a big green accounting book which our CPA insists we keep in case we are ever audited again by the Internal Revenue Service. I pulled up a chair at the breakfast table, ran my fingers gingerly over the depression in the wall thinking I needed to get some kind of decorative plaque to cover it and opened my Bible to the Book of Jonah.

As I said, it is a short book. Four chapters long. Most of the story is familiar. Jonah receiving a call from God to preach in Nineveh. His running from God. The incident aboard the ship when he is finally thrown overboard. That infamous whale. Then Jonah picking himself up off the beach and, reeking of seaweed and caviar, heading out to Nineveh to preach the Word of the Lord.

But it was the rest of the story Jackie wanted me to read—and I did so with some care. It seems that when a prophet with seaweed in his hair shows up and preaches repentance, people take him seriously. Not only did the people repent, but so did the king. They all put on sackcloth, smeared themselves in ashes, and God honored their repentance and withheld His judgment.

Then Jonah went outside the city, and that's where the difficult part of the story commences. Jonah was angry. He was angry because his theology had been shaken. It seems Jonah, the Jew, felt all

Assyrians deserved to be destroyed. In fact, he was hoping they would not repent and he could sit outside the city and watch as God wiped them out with fire and brimstone. When the destruction was withheld, however, Jonah grew angry and cried out to God to take his life.

One of the best ways to discover what a man is really like is to discover what makes him angry. I guess that was the reason Jackie wanted me to read about Jonah—because it seems his anger was simply evidence of some other things inside him which were all messed up.

I paused as I read, thinking about the incident at lunch. It was just one of many, for I get angry at a lot of things. Big things seldom make me angry. It is the little things which cause me to blow my top. Just let someone scratch the surface of my life, upset my pet plan, disrupt my routine, interfere with my . . . everything seemed to be centered around the word "my." Just as it was with Jonah. He had come to Nineveh with a chip on his shoulder. He was prejudiced. He had hated the Assyrians all his life. After all, the Jews were God's chosen people—not the Arabs. Had it not been for that storm at sea and God's indisputable direction for his life, he would have been safe in Tarshish. Even so, he arrived in Nineveh convinced he was right—and they were wrong. He could not handle it when they became right too.

I thought ahead. What made Jesus angry? Or better, what didn't make Him angry? They tried to stone Him at Nazareth, right after He made His purpose known in public. That didn't make Him angry.

He did not become angry when He was feeding the 5,000, and His disciples didn't have any faith.

He did not become angry when He beckoned the men to walk on water with Him and only Peter had enough gumption to try it. Nor did He become angry when Peter lost his faith and began to sink.

He was not angry at the religious leaders when they rejected His healing miracles.

He was not angry when a group of men disrupted the preaching services and took the roof off and spilled dirt and debris all over the pulpit. It didn't seem to bother Him that they were tearing up someone's property.

He wasn't even angry when His disciples—after three years of teaching—asked Him stupid questions. Just the night before He died, Phillip interrupted one of His most profound teachings by saying, "We don't know what you're talking about. You keep talking about the way to the Father. We don't even know who the Father is, much less the way."

Jesus answered back so gently. Patiently. "You mean you've been with me for three years and do not know that I am the way—the truth and the life? And if you've seen me, you've seen the Father. For we are of the same spirit." No anger. Just eternal patience.

Even when the men who were closest to Him went to sleep in the garden after He asked them to watch for those who would come to arrest Him, He was not angry. Nor was He angry when they all fled—leaving Him alone. He was not even angry when He was falsely accused, mocked, beaten, and finally hung up on a cross to die. He was often sad. Sometimes, it seems, disappointed. But seldom angry.

What did make Him angry?

He was angry when the Pharisees, the religious leaders of the day, took cruel advantage of the poor, of widows and orphans. The entire 23rd chapter of Matthew is a fierce diatribe against people who act religious but are not spiritual at heart.

In the 25th chapter of Matthew, He was angry. Here it was a different kind of anger. He was angry at a man who did not use what he had been given for the glory of God. He called him wicked and slothful.

Another time He was passing down the road and spotted a fig tree covered with leaves but producing no figs. He cursed the tree and it died. His anger then was toward those who held out promises but made no pretense at delivering.

And of course there was that famous scene in the Temple the week before He was crucified when He drove out the moneychangers who had taken the house of prayer and turned it into a den of thieves and robbers. He was really angry that time. Yet He turned right around and healed both a blind man and a crippled man in the Temple.

I came back to Jonah, sitting under a big leafy gourd vine which God had caused to grow up almost instantaneously to give him shade. Now Jonah was angry again. This time because a big green worm came along, ate the vine and caused it to die—taking away his shade.

No wonder Jackie wanted me to read the last chapter of Jonah. That could have been me, sitting out there in the hot Assyrian sun. I'm angry at the Assyrians because they repented. I'm angry at God for not wiping them out. I'm angry at the worm. I'm angry at myself because I can't control my anger.

How like Jonah I was. How unlike Jesus.

I sat there in the kitchen at the breakfast table, looking up at the dent in the wall. At least Jonah had finally obeyed God and gone to preach to the Assyrians. And I hadn't done anything but lose my temper and bust my wife's best salt shaker all over the kitchen.

I could see her in the dining room, poring over those books. Her check stubs were scattered all over the table. Bills and receipts were in little piles on the floor nearby. It was 9:30 P.M. on a Friday, and she had been going since 6 A.M. when she got up to get breakfast for the children before they left for school. I felt a hot wave of shame sweep through me. How stupid can a man be? Here God had given me something far more valuable than Jonah's gourd vine—the most wonderful wife in the world—and I showed my appreciation by smashing her salt shaker against the wall. *Some man of God you are. You're more like those whited sepulchers Jesus condemned than God's man of faith and power.*

So getting out pencil and paper, I decided to use the rest of the evening, while Jackie was balancing the books, listing the things that made me angry and why. It was quite an experience.

First of all, I discovered that I seldom got angry at the things which made Jesus angry. Next I discovered that the things which made me angry were legion. I got angry at a whole lot of things. As a matter of fact, I spent a great portion of my life being angry at something—or someone.

Shortly afterwards I heard Jackie sigh as she closed her ledger, pushed back her chair and came into the kitchen. She stood at the sink for a few moments, letting the water run over her hands, then dried them with a paper towel and came over to where I was at the table.

"Reading Jonah?"

"How'd you guess?"

"Well, I figured you were when I saw you making a list."

"Oh?" I felt the back of my neck growing red.

"I'll bet you're making a list of all the things that make you angry, aren't you?"

I was really blushing by this time. I tried to cover my list. "You think you know me pretty well, don't you?"

"I'm not as stupid as you think," she chuckled. "Let me see your list. I'll bet I can add some things you've left off."

I flushed with anger as she reached for my list. I yanked it away.

"See? There's one I'll bet you didn't add. 'I get angry when my wife looks over my shoulder.' "

I sighed, shook my head in resignation and pushed the list at her. "Go ahead. I might as well be hung up naked before the world."

She reached out, rubbed the back of my neck and the tops of my shoulders in a gesture that always brings peace. "Why don't we work on this together? Instead of your making a list, let me make one for you. And you make one for me."

Now that was something I could really get my teeth into.

It turned out to be a remarkably revealing procedure. I recommend it only if you can stand the white light of honesty and then only if the one making the list knows you well enough—and loves you well enough—to list everything. I guess, if I lived with my mother, I could have asked her to do it. (Although I'm not so sure she would have been as devastatingly honest as my wife—and I am certain she would not have enjoyed it as much.) As it was, Jackie seemed to enjoy listing—with my approval—all the things that, in her opinion, made me angry.

And I, in turn, thought it was a great opportunity for me to point out some of her anger points.

My list of things which made Jackie angry included:

—when I lie to her—and she finds it out;

—when I interrupt her while she's talking;

—my refusal to discipline the children;

—my refusal to back her up when she disciplines the children;

—when I leave the car windows open at night and it rains in and gets the seat wet and she has to take the children to school;

—when I invite people home to lunch—or home to spend a month as our guests—without asking her first;

—when some other woman makes a play for me;

—when I respond to some other woman who makes a play for me;

—when I promise to take her someplace special and then cancel out to help someone else;

—especially if that "someone else" is another woman.

Her list of the things which make me angry was much longer. It included things like:

—interruptions;

—incompetence (in the men around you or the wife beside you);

—intolerance;

—messiness (such as someone leaving the cap off the toothpaste or not wringing out a wet wash cloth);

—sickness;

—name droppers;

—injustice;

—laziness (such as when one of your fellow workers puts off an assigned task or when one of the children doesn't return the tools after they have used them);

—criticism by your wife;

—when your wife disagrees with you in public;

—betrayal;

—cruelty;

—compromise;

—liars;

—when you are caught in a lie;

—stinginess;

—ingratitude;

—egotistical persons;

—when your wife refuses to get you out of the mess you've gotten yourself into;

174

—blasphemy;
—lack of courtesy to a woman (unless it is your wife);
—your own ineptness.

I sat for a long time looking at her list—the one she had made about me. She was right in most instances. But some of them puzzled me.

"What's this bit about 'sickness'?" I asked. "What do you mean I get angry at sickness?"

"Oh, I don't mean sickness per se," she answered. "I mean you get angry when I get sick."

I've given a lot of thought to that. The Lord is forever revealing new areas of hard-heartedness in my spirit, and that is one of them. I recall, when I first entered the ministry, there were mornings when my young pregnant wife would be too sick to get out of bed. That meant I had to be late to work, staying home in order to fix breakfast for the children, get them dressed and clean up the house. That smoldering anger built up in me, and since I was not able to express it against the busybodies who were constantly checking but never helping, I vented it against my wife. "If you wouldn't get sick in the morning, you could do the housework, and I could get on to my office and be busy with the important things of God."

At first she reacted in anger. "If you hadn't gotten me pregnant, I wouldn't be sick!"

Later she gave in under my relentless attacks and would say softly, "Have you ever considered that your wife and children might be just as much the 'work of God' as sticking pins in maps in the church office, making sure the financial statements are mailed out and preparing the church bulletin?"

However, like all priests and Levites, it is hard to see the importance of binding up wounds when there are duties awaiting at the Temple. So I passed her by on the other side, fuming all the while at her occasional spells of morning sickness.

Across the years I learned to modulate my anger, to keep it under control. But it was there all the time, smoldering. Every time Jackie was sick, even though I no longer fussed about it,

175

she could sense that deep attitude of anger which was always present in my spirit. What right did she have to get sick? Did she not realize that her sickness prevented me from doing important things and interfered with my way of life?

As I examined this one point, I realized that my anger, like so many other emotions, centered around and grew out of my self-centeredness. Jonah was angry because the worm destroyed his shade. He was angry because it was his prejudices which were called into question. I got angry at Jackie because her sickness, or her needs, disturbed the things I wanted to do. Incompetence on the part of those around me caused me to be angry because that meant I had to do not only my job but theirs as well. It all grew out of my self-centeredness.

Recently I got up early on Sunday morning, as I usually do, and disappeared into my studio in a far wing of the house to prepare myself spiritually and mentally for the Sunday morning service. Jackie and the children like to sleep later on Sundays, but I usually rise early, do some physical exercises, perhaps take a walk through the pine trees and then go into my study to make final notes for my teaching session at the morning service. I deliberately separate myself from the family and the normal confusion that goes along with getting ready for church so as to be in just the right frame of mind to teach the Word.

On that particular Sunday morning, I had followed the normal routine and emerged from my studio at precisely the moment we should get in the car and drive to church. As usual, I expected all the children to be perfectly dressed and sitting in the car, waiting for me to get in behind the wheel and drive us to church, singing and praising the Lord all the way.

Of course it never happened that way, but I found it better to have an unattainable goal than no standard at all. This particular Sunday morning things were worse than usual. Tim was still in the shower. Sandy was upstairs curling her hair. Jackie had opened the refrigerator door to get some milk for the cat, and a big bowl of jello had crashed to the floor. Our oldest son, Bruce, had just pulled up in the driveway announcing he was leaving his little two-seater car for us to drive to church so he could borrow the

176

station wagon for a youth picnic, and the phone was ringing. One of our daughters, away at college, was calling to ask for money. It took about 20 seconds for me to evaluate the situation and lose all the spirituality I had been working on since six that morning. I stormed around a little, did some shouting, popped a button off my shirt and finally announced that everyone could get to church on their own; I was taking the car and leaving.

Halfway down the drive I had second thoughts and returned to wait for the family. It turned out we were still on time, but the tornado of anger which roared through my life and out again had left me washed out—empty. When I stood that morning and confessed my anger and asked how many others in the congregation had gone through similar situations, the show of hands indicated I was in the majority. Fortunately, God took my weakness and converted it to His strength—and gave us all a new revelation that morning about self-centeredness.

Anger is an effect. And for every effect there is a cause. The cause of anger is not hate. The basic cause of anger is fear. Our anger is a façade we raise to hide our insecurities. So when Paul tells Timothy that God has not given us a spirit of fear but of power and of love and of a sound mind—he wipes out all the reasons for self-anger.

All anger is not wrong, of course. The Bible talks a great deal about the anger of God. But God never got angry in relative situations. He was angry only in the area of absolutes. He never struck out at that which was relatively wrong, only against that which was absolutely wrong. What we often call losing our temper really means we have given way to the things which control us: insecurity, fear, jealousy, self-centeredness. Our "temper" is nothing more than the control valve which keeps us in check. But the man under full control of the Holy Spirit is no longer in subjection to the whims, feelings, appetites, passions and lusts which formerly controlled his life. Now all these are in subjection to the higher power of God working within. Instead of being a slave to your anger, anger becomes your servant—a tool in your hands to accomplish good things.

Last year we had a little situation develop which centered around

177

our 15-year-old daughter, Sandy. One afternoon she came home from junior high school, where she was finishing the ninth grade, and announced that Thursday, May 25, was "Freshman Skip Day" at Johnson Junior High School.

I asked her the normal questions. Is this an allowable skip day? Is the school approving? Will she be excused? She answered no to all the questions. If it was allowable it wouldn't be any fun. Half the fun came in doing something which was against the rules. However, she reminded me, Freshman Skip Day was an old and honorable tradition. For years the graduating class at the junior high had participated in skip day. The school officials always knew it was coming and always made a big commotion about it, threatening to suspend any student who skipped, but in the end they always laughed, winked and took it in stride. "Besides," she asked me, "didn't you have a skip day when you were in school back in the 'roaring '20s'?"

I reminded her I wasn't even born during the "roaring '20s," but yes, we did have skip day, and yes, I guessed it would be all right for her to participate since it was an old and honorable tradition.

There were several things I did not know. One of them was the new principal at the junior high school was formerly an assistant superintendent of public education and was not in sympathy at all with skip day, or with any other old and honorable tradition which pulled kids out of school. The other thing I did not know was Sandy had invited all the kids in her class to come out to our house for a swimming party on skip day.

Two weeks before the infamous skip day was to take place, Sandy came home from school very excited. Someone had squealed. The officials had discovered that Thursday, May 25—a day which was supposed to be ultra-secret—was scheduled by the junior high underground as skip day. The rumor was spreading through the school that a number of police officers had been assigned to stations all over the city to arrest the kids as they skipped and put them in jail. So they had a little caucus meeting after school that day and changed skip day from Thursday to Friday. That made it even more fun.

By that time it was too late to back out, and Sandy then told us she had invited a number of her friends out to our house on skip day to swim in the pool. We had no choice but to go along. We insisted, however, that any child who came to our house had to bring a note from the parents granting permission.

Friday, May 26, about 40 ninth-grade children appeared in our back yard—nearly all of them chauffeured by their parents. They were a well-behaved group and all had permission notes. They had brought sack lunches and, after receiving instructions from Jackie on what to do and what not to do in the pool, began their party. They seemed to be having a great time and Jackie left to run some errands, leaving me at home with the 40 kids. Our college-age daughter, Bonnie, was home at the time and agreed to act as the lifeguard.

I returned to my studio and was at work at my desk when I looked out the window and saw children running everywhere. Still dressed in their bathing suits, they were fleeing across the pasture and dashing out into the woods. I leaped up and ran outside only to be met by Bonnie, running toward the house with a breathless expression on her face.

"The principal and the dean of the school are here. They just pulled up in the front driveway."

I glanced around the corner of the house and sure enough, there came the principal of the school. And he had the dean with him—marching across the yard toward the swimming pool. They looked angry. The kids were still fleeing in all directions.

Before I knew it I, too, was fleeing. Back into the house. Up the stairs. It wasn't until I got in the upstairs clothes closet that I realized, *Hey, this is stupid! Why am I running and hiding? This is my house. I live here. I own this house. Why should I flee from the principal and the dean?*

Sheepishly I came back down the stairs, gave Bonnie, who was peeking around the corner of the den, a crooked grin and opened the front door. There were the two school officials. Sullen and angry. I invited them in and we had a little conversation. The principal was very pointed. "I want you to know that what's happened here is strictly against the school board rules. This is not allowed. You are aiding and abetting criminals in your house."

I really didn't know what to do, since legally he was right. I

179

told him I was sorry he felt that way and even more sorry he didn't have a skip day when he was 15 years old. Looking at him, I suspected that he never had been 15 years old, but nevertheless I respected his authority and promised to send the children away.

After he left, I went back outside and called all the children together. I explained the principal was under the authority of the law, and I was under the authority of the principal, and they were under my authority, and they had to leave. They thought it was kind of fun that they had been caught and all came in and called their parents who came after them.

When it was all over, I went back in the house and sat down at my typewriter. My fingers were still shaking from the whole episode. I asked myself, *Why am I afraid of the principal?* After all these years of being out of school, all someone had to say was, "The principal and the dean are here," and I ran and hid.

It relates to fear. Fear of principals, deans and truant officers was built into me as a child. It is still with me. That fear of authority often eventuates itself in anger against authority figures. Once I grasped the fact that it was my house, that I lived there, that whoever was knocking at my door—even if it was the principal—could come in only on my invitation, then I was fine. But until that time, I had been running and hiding like all the rest of the children. Afraid.

People who are offended easily, who are edgy when someone or something rubs them the wrong way, who put up angry defense mechanisms, are usually very insecure, self-centered individuals. We don't want people getting close to us for fear they will discover what we are really like. Discovering that, we are afraid they won't like us any more. It is easier just to get angry.

As Christians come together in community, true koinonia, there will be even more rubbing and touching. We often reject this, afraid that if we are rubbed hard enough, others will discover we are only a thin veneer or that we're hollow inside. But it is only when the masks come off, when the outer layers are discarded, that we can be filled—and eventually, controlled—by the Holy Spirit. The purpose of our being rubbed and sandpapered and chiseled is not to expose us but to open us. A man cannot expand in the spirit if he has 19 coats of paint on him. Wineskins with that kind of covering never can hold the effervescing new wine.

Crusty people, those who get angry easily, are usually stiff and unbending. They have no elasticity. When confronted with situations they cannot handle, they blow up. Blood vessels in their head pop. Or their heart explodes. Or a stomach or colon ruptures or develops an ulcer. The Holy Spirit, however, is the spirit of health. His desire, in controlling us, is to bring us to that place where everything works in harmony with the Lord of the universe—our heavenly Father.

The week after my experience with Jonah, I hung a plaque over that big dent on the breakfast room wall. In the process, the Lord spoke, in the deep area of my heart, and said, "It's all right to hang the plaque, but I want you to remember what it's covering— and how it got there. I want you to remember you are still an angry person who can't control himself. You need the daily control of my Holy Spirit."

Recently I dropped a little note to the wife of a well-known minister who lived out of state. Her husband's newsletter, which I receive, had mentioned an incident in which his wife and her parents had been involved. It was an interesting experience, and I was eager for a little more detail. So I wrote her a note and asked if she would send me full details on the incident her husband had alluded to in his newsletter. At the bottom of the letter, I penned a P.S. which said, "By the way, if you are ever in need of a place of retreat or if you need a shoulder to cry on, Jackie and I would like to invite you to spend a few days in our guest house in Florida."

I didn't think anything about it, for it's an invitation I have given to several others. Ministers' wives, I have discovered, sometimes need to get away from home—and their husbands—for a few days. Two weeks later I got a blistering letter back from my friend, the woman's husband. Not only was he angry, but he was deeply offended. What right did I have to insinuate that he could not take care of all his wife's needs? Didn't I recognize him as her spiritual covering? Didn't I recognize he provided everything she needed? It was a very angry letter.

I spent four days answering that letter. I threw the first five or six answers in the trash, and finally I wrote one that Jackie could approve—one which did not psychoanalyze my brother and point out his reasons for being angry. But the question needs to be faced sometime. Why are we so easily offended? Why do we react with so much anger when things don't go exactly our way? Why will a housewife invariably snap at one child but treat another child gently? Why, when someone comes along and suggests a change in our life style, do we grow angry? Why would a minister assume I had accused him of being less than Mr. Everything to his wife—unless he was indeed deficient? Why have some of you reading this book gotten angry?

Last year I was invited by the pastor of a Presbyterian church in Atlanta to share with his session some of the new concepts being revealed by the Holy Spirit. I tried to be gentle and kind. I told them the story about the ruts in the Sinai. But even as I talked, I sensed one man in the back of the room was building up a full head of steam. His face was blanched and there was a little white ring around his mouth—a sure sign of a coming explosion. When I finished speaking, I opened the floor for questions or discussion. He was the first one on his feet, his eyes narrow, his voice shaking as he talked.

"I am highly offended," he said. "You have come into my church—the church my father belonged to, the church my grandfather helped build—and said we need to change our ways. Well, I want to tell you right now, I'm damn well pleased with the way we're doing things, and I don't intend to change."

Then he sat down.

Fortunately, he was the only one in the room who seemed to feel that way. Immediately others came rushing to my defense and by the time we finished the evening his ruffled feathers were smoothed. But underneath his anger, I knew, was a huge vacuum of insecurity, and I had almost taken away the shroud and exposed him to himself—and his peers. No wonder he had exploded. It was his only defense.

There is a fine line between self-centeredness and self-confidence, between egotism and security. The insecure man is always afraid.

182

The secure man, the man who knows who he is and is unashamed of his flaws—for he has faced them and confessed them long before the accuser gets to him—may be frightened on occasion but never afraid.

In the flyleaf of my Bible I have written a number of messages to myself—personal messages from God to me. One of them says: "Jamie, don't let the world—or the church—mold you into its image." Some of my friends do not understand my sometimes strange ways, but I am determined to hear and do the will of God for me—despite what others think I should do. This does not mean I do not fail and need the correction and adjustment of others. But it does mean that I shall not be ashamed—or afraid—of my imperfections. And I shall push on, despite my flaws, and present my body a living sacrifice, blemishes and all, and believe I am acceptable to His service. For it is far better to risk and fail than to count myself unworthy and not risk at all.

That means I must be willing to be myself—and live with others' anger and not grow angry in return.

One of the areas of my life which is constantly under examination is my relationship with tomatoes. I do not eat them. I never have eaten a tomato. This is not necessarily a religious practice, it is just that I cannot stand the thought of biting into one of those quivering, jellied, nauseating things. It is not that I have anything against tomatoes per se, for I love catsup. I eat catsup on everything from cheese to scrambled eggs. But a long time ago I made a quality decision—and for the life of me I do not know why—that I would not eat tomatoes. The thought of biting into one of them is as repulsive as biting into an earthworm. That's just the way I am.

I almost ate one several years ago. I had ordered a hamburger at a hamburger stand ("Skip the tomatoes, please") and took it back to my table. I had already taken a bite when I discovered I had that awful thing in my mouth. It wasn't the thought of swallowing the tomato which bothered me, it was the thought of chewing it up. Fortunately I was able to spit it out. Then I had to go through the process of getting it off my hamburger before it soaked into the bun—all those little seeds with mucus around them. Then

I discovered I had gotten some of it on my fork and had to wipe it off—much to the pleasure of my children who were watching and giggling. However, I maintained my virginity and can proudly state to this day I have never eaten a tomato (which some theologians, I understand, believe was the fruit Eve gave Adam in the Garden, thus contaminating all mankind).

It doesn't bother me that I don't eat tomatoes. I am not the least bit embarrassed to take the tomatoes out of my salad and put them in my wife's bowl when we go out to eat. I pick them out of the soup as well, for the only thing worse than a raw tomato is a cooked one—especially if it is boiled with okra. Just as I do not drink hard liquor, snort cocaine, dip snuff, sprinkle voodoo dust in my bellybutton or chant incantations to the devil—so I do not eat tomatoes. It is simply part of my way of living and comes as natural as saying "no thank you" when asked if I want a martini or a whiskey sour.

But while some of my Christian friends may applaud my abstinence from hard liquor, very few of them understand my decision to skip tomatoes.

"What? You don't like tomatoes? What's wrong with you anyway?"

"What are you doing, taking all the tomatoes out of your salad?"

"You eat catsup, don't you? What's the difference?"

I've heard these and every other remark during the 47 years I have not eaten tomatoes. The difference is I have chosen not to eat tomatoes. That's my way of life. I do not grow angry when questioned. I am secure. I am satisfied to remain that way.

The other day I visited the cafeteria in Vero Beach with my mother, my wife and a lady missionary friend the same age as my mother. We went through the line and I ordered a piece of ground steak. The woman behind the counter asked if I wanted mushroom sauce on it. I said yes. I didn't know the mushrooms were cooked in tomatoes and before I knew it she had smeared that awful stuff all over my meat—big hunks of quivering, pink tomato in lots of juice. I took it calmly and when we got to our table I began, as unobtrusively as possible, to take the tomatoes off my meat and put them on the bread plate. Well, the ladies at the table thought that was awful. All of them had loud things to say about my not liking tomatoes. My mother said it was a shame I was still like that. My wife said I embarrassed her every time I went to a restaurant. The elderly missionary lady said if I lived overseas long enough I'd learn to eat things like that—and be grateful. I managed to smile through it all and finally wound up pouring the tomato juice into the ashtray on the table to keep it from soaking into my cornbread. I enjoyed my dinner immensely, but the ladies never did seem to get back in the mood for eating.

In the areas where I am secure, where I know who I am and where I am going (such as in the area of my relationship with the despicable tomato), I never grow angry. In such areas I refuse to let the world—even the world of my wife and mother—mold me into its image. It is only when I am on shaky ground, unsure of my stance or afraid to take off my mask and let folks see me the way I really am, that I explode in the defense mechanism of anger.

Salvation, in its purest sense, is becoming the person you really are—the person God created you to be. It is possible, I can report, to live above the humanism of this world and to achieve the individuality and personal identity with God that each man yearns for. But it can be done only when a man comes to grips with the fact he is different, that God has a unique place and purpose for him in life, and he does not need to defend his status—just live it out.

A few years ago I was invited to be one of the principal speakers for a major Episcopal convention in Kansas City. It was quite an honor since I was appearing on the program with two bishops and the dean of a cathedral. Pretty high company for a defrocked Baptist who doesn't even like to wear a necktie. Several days before I was to fly to Kansas City, I bumped into an old friend, the esteemed rector of one of the Episcopal Churches in our city. I was to be the baccalaureate speaker at our local high school again, and the priest was also on the program. We had a few moments before the processional began in the high school gymnasium and he said, "I see where you are to be in high company this coming week."

"How did you know?" I asked.

"Oh, I saw it in one of the brochures."

"I have no idea why they asked me," I said honestly, and a little apologetically. "I'm the only non-Anglican in the line-up."

The priest grinned and said, "Oh, I know why they invited you. Because you painted out your sign."

It was time for us to move to the platform. I was still trying to figure out what he was talking about. Then I remembered. Several years before, when our church was just breaking out of some of the traditional ruts and heading across the desert, we put a sign beside the main road with an arrow which pointed toward our modest building. Feeling that every church needed some kind of slogan, we painted one on the sign. It said: "For those who want more than a Sunday religion."

Several months later one of our elders approached me. "I was in an interdenominational meeting this week," he said. "Some of the people from the Episcopal church were present. One of them told me, in a kind but firm way, that our slogan offended him— and a number of others in the parish as well. He said he didn't see anything wrong with a Sunday religion, and he was disappointed we seemed to be capitalizing on a cheap dig at their beliefs."

My first impulse was to shrug and say, "Tough luck." But that afternoon as I stood in my study, I glanced at another slogan, this one hanging in a frame on my wall. It was a needlepoint gift from some admirer who had heard me use the phrase at some conference, had stitched it beautifully on a piece of cloth, then shipped it to me in a frame. It had been hanging above my typewriter for several months. It said simply:

"It is better to be kind than to be right."

I evaluated that in the light of what I had just heard. My first reaction had been anger. The slogan on our sign was right. Our faith needs to be more than a Sunday religion. Actually, as I thought about it, I knew the priest believed that also. But he is a staunch sacramentalist and to him the most important event of the week is that which takes place when the sacraments are administered to the people. In fact, to him nothing has meaning during the week except that which is related in a dynamic way to the serving

186

of the sacraments. Even though I do not totally agree with that, I deeply respect his position and was eager to move even closer to it. But how could I do that if I was deliberately offending all the sacramentalists in our community with our sign? After all, while my concepts of rightness are a matter of relativity, there is nothing relative about kindness. It is an absolute command from the Holy Spirit.

And be ye kind one to another, tenderhearted, forgiving one another, even as God for Christ's sake hath forgiven you (Ephesians 4:32).

So I had asked someone to paint out the slogan. That's what the priest was referring to. Now the bread I had cast on the waters had come back, and I was to speak to the very group I had earlier offended.

There comes a time in the life of every Spirit-baptized Christian when he has to face the fact that character is more important than charisma. Charisma is a gift to us from God while character is a trait required of us by God. Character means turning the other cheek when slapped. It means walking the second mile after we are forced by another to walk the first. It means giving up our shirt after someone has forced us to give our coat. It means not eating meat or drinking wine in the presence of one who feels these things are wrong. It means reaching out to heal when everything within us says we should slash out with a sword in self-righteous anger.

This kind of character is dangerous, for it makes us vulnerable to the attack of others. There is an interesting story which appears in all four gospels concerning the night Jesus was arrested in the Garden of Gethsemane. Jesus had been praying while His disciples slept. Suddenly the garden was lighted with torches as soldiers and Temple guards came rushing in, led by Judas, to arrest the Son of God. There was very little warning before the soldiers were upon Him. Hearing the disturbance, Simon Peter leaped to his feet and drew his sword. Seeing Malthus, the bodyguard for Annas, the high priest, approaching Jesus, Peter stepped forward and with a single blow of his sword cut off the ear of the armed henchman.

Doubtless Peter intended to cut off his head, but in his sleepy condition he missed.

Jesus then stepped forward, laid His hand on Peter's muscular arm, and said softly, "That's not necessary, Peter. Put away your sword. If I needed to be defended, I could call 10,000 angels."

Then, reaching out to Malthus, He touched the side of his head where blood was gushing out and healed him. It was an extremely delicate moment. The angry Temple guard had already drawn his sword. Peter's wound had made him even angrier. And into this situation stepped the Son of God, exposing His chest as He reached out toward the wounded one. Perhaps Malthus sensed he was in the presence of God. Perhaps he was too shocked to move. The normal reaction would have been to thrust his short sword into the chest of the man who was reaching for him, for it is at that moment of healing that God's people are most vulnerable. But the soft word turned away the wrath of anger.

Here we are, busy defending the Gospel with our sword of the Spirit, slashing in all directions as we declare our rightness. Then comes Jesus, touching ears and healing. Running the risk of being killed—because it is better to be kind than to be right.

Anger is a barrier that blocks relationships. But until I can identify it as such, I will not be able to relate correctly to those I wish to heal. Thus I must constantly ask myself if I am willing to undergo periods of discomfort, even make myself vulnerable to pain and death, in order to bring about change. The self-expressionist says, "Don't inhibit yourself. If you feel it, do it." But it is far better to act your way into a feeling, than to feel your way into a course of action. In this case you can, by a deliberate act, expose yourself to the power of the Holy Spirit who will take that which you cannot control, bring it under His control and use it as a tool for the glory of God.

XI

Kissing Frogs

Perhaps my friend the prophet, Bruce Morgan, is right when he says, "The trouble with Christians is no one wants to kill them anymore."

Every place the Apostle Paul went, there was a revival or a riot. Today's seminaries teach a lot of good things, but few of them teach Christians how to react when rioted against—especially if the Christian is the instigator.

Maybe such things can't be taught and must be caught instead. But very few Christians seem interested these days in getting spit on.

Mike Evans, founder of the B'nai Yeshua Center on Long Island, sponsors a national conference for Messianic Jews called *Shechinah*. Last year's conference was to feature Ruth Stapleton, the sister of President Jimmy Carter, as the keynote speaker. The significance of her appearance and the recognition it would have provided for the evangelistic effort among Jews was too much to go unchallenged. Powerful Jewish and Christian political organizations combined to exert great pressure—and forced her to cancel out at the last minute.

Discouraged, Mike Evans called me at my home in Florida, wondering if he should call off the conference. I suggested he should first examine his motives. Maybe God wanted to send a prophet instead of a princess.

Mike agreed, and invited me.

I accepted and got spit on.

There were about 1,500 present that opening night—most of them Messianic Jews, some of them former rabbis. About 10 minutes into my message, 20 militant young demonstrators jumped to their feet and stormed the platform, shouting slogans like, "Death to Jews for Jesus!" All were members of the Jewish Defense League, led by the National Student Coordinator.

It was a nasty scene. They took over the platform and threatened to cut the microphone wires if not allowed to speak. The police were there, but Mike wisely refused to let them arrest the demonstrators. The more the JDL youth shouted hate and death slogans, the more the people in the audience responded by shouting, "We love you!" When the demonstrators began singing a lively Jewish song, the audience joined in, clapping and dancing the hora. They then went on to sing another six stanzas of the same song which the demonstrators didn't know. The demonstrators had obviously hoped to be handcuffed and dragged bleeding from the stage while the news photographers and TV cameras (which had appeared mysteriously out of the night) snapped their pictures. But none of this happened. Finally Mike agreed to let the leader speak for five minutes if he would then leave peacefully. Fortunately, his threats were captured on the still-running tape recorder.

"This house of slime, this house of profanity will never be allowed to exist. This is just the beginning of the JDL campaign to eradicate the bastard movement. We consider you whores and traitors to your people. This is just the beginning. The burning of this building will be the end."

The group then marched offstage, shaking their fists—but not before someone spit on me, the only *goy* on the platform.

The next morning the New York *Times* carried the story, along with the accusation from the leader that all those people at B'nai Yeshua had been paid $10 a person to love—for no one loves without being paid for it.

He was closer to the truth than he suspected.

It's the business of the church to love—even when you get spit on.

Ironically, one of the classic statements on love (even though the word is never mentioned) was written by the German pastor, Martin Niemoller, one of the outstanding Protestant scholars in Europe during World War II. In writing about the political and religious persecution of the Jews in Nazi Germany, Niemoller stated: "In Germany the Nazis came for the Communists, and I didn't speak up because I was not a Communist. Then they came for the Jews and I didn't speak up because I was not a Jew. Then they came for the Trade Unionists and I didn't speak up because I wasn't a Trade Unionist. Then they came for the Catholics and I was a Protestant so I didn't speak up. Then they came for me— but by that time there was no one to speak up for anyone."

We are not only our brother's keeper, we are our brother's lover— even when he spits on us.

Three weeks later I was speaking at Gerald Derstine's beautiful Christian Retreat in Bradenton, Florida. The second night I poked a little fun at some of Christendom's sacred cows—the idols we set up. After the service I was standing at the front of the auditorium shaking hands with a number of people who gathered around. There was a lot of love flowing when suddenly I was face to face with a stocky, serious-faced woman in her early 50s. Her graying hair was pulled back and tied tightly in a bun. She wore no makeup and her face was hard, her eyes flashing anger.

"You are a servant of the devil," she said loudly.

Suddenly everything was deathly still. She continued, "How dare you make fun of the cross around my neck and the dove on my license plate? Jesus died on this cross. God sent that dove to bring His Holy Spirit."

I should have kept my mouth shut. "Lady, Jesus didn't die on that cross. That cross is made of gold, and you bought it from some moneychanger in the temple."

It was then she spit on me. A great big spit which clung briefly to the lapel of my coat and then dribbled down toward my shoe.

"Why don't you give us the Word instead of all this garbage?" she sneered, and then stalked off in the direction of Gerald who

191

was standing in the back of the auditorium. I hoped, for his sake, she was out of spit.

"Now what are you supposed to do?" a sympathetic woman asked as she handed me a kleenex.

"I'm supposed to wait until she stops croaking," I said seriously. "Then I'll go up and kiss her. Who knows, perhaps she'll turn into a princess."

Everyone laughed, and the fellowship was restored. But it's more than a laughing matter. The story of the handsome prince who came under the spell of the wicked witch and was turned into a frog—redeemable only through a kiss—is far more spiritual truth than a fairy tale. There are a lot of froggy people in this world, not a few of whom are in the church. The only way they can be transformed is for someone who has a lot to lose, like a Christian, to see the potential beneath their frogginess and kiss them into their inheritance.

But in kissing frogs, the Christian makes himself vulnerable. There is always the danger the frog will spit on you—or even worse. It may be the frog is not a handsome prince at all but just a frog keeping a tally sheet of suckers.

Yet we must keep on bending, stooping, kissing and hoping. Sometimes it's the frog himself who objects. "I'm poison; kiss me and you'll die too." Or perhaps he's a liberated frog who says, "I don't want to be a prince. I only want self-fulfillment as an amphibian." Other times the pressure comes from those around us who are too dignified to stoop and kiss and are threatened by our serving posture. But someone must run the risk, for there is no other way this ugly, froggy old earth will be redeemed.

Under the warts is the image of God. It has been covered by sin and hardened, often, by those who came in the name of the church with whips rather than the balm of Gilead. But the potential of kingship remains and can be released only through someone willing to bend, stoop and kiss.

Our life pattern is Jesus, who was the greatest frog kisser of all. He gave up His exalted place in heaven to walk among us as a servant, to wash dirty feet, receive our spit and our spears and in a final act of supreme grace to send His Holy Spirit to fill the very ones who rejected Him so they could carry on the work He began—kissing frogs.

The young JDL leader said it's unnatural to love. He's right. Only those whose lives are controlled by another Spirit will do such foolish things as turn the other cheek, walk the second mile, join an enemy in song (and teach him an extra stanza or two) and stoop to kiss frogs.

Why, one will hardly die for a righteous man—though perhaps for a good man one will dare even to die. But God shows his love for us in that while we were yet sinners [*while we were yet spitting on him*] Christ died for us (Romans 5:7–8, RSV).

That's the ultimate in kissing frogs.

Can men of God, despite pride and rigidity, do less?

There is so much we do not understand about the ways of God, especially why everything in the Kingdom seems so upside down to our way of thinking. Bruce Morgan is right when he says if we continued to live by the law which says an eye for an eye and a tooth for a tooth, we'd soon create a blind and toothless generation. God has a better way—the way of grace. Yet even this defies description and explanation—at least from man's point of view.

The prophet Habakkuk, hundreds of years before Christ, spent a good portion of his life trying to figure out why God allows people to be turned into frogs in the first place. Habakkuk's little book is composed of two long complaints and a sigh of resignation. Habakkuk didn't like the way God was running the universe, especially with the way He was dealing with His chosen people, Israel. It didn't seem right that God was going to destroy His own nation, even if they were wicked. Especially was Habakkuk upset that God was using a nation even more wicked than Judah to do His dirty work for Him. God answered Habakkuk's complaint with a simple statement of fact, saying in essence, "O man of this earth, you don't know what you're talking about. True, I am sending the Chaldeans to destroy the nation of Judah. But take comfort, for in turn the Chaldeans will be destroyed also."

That didn't seem to comfort the prophet very much. It was like saying, "Yes, that mob is going to burn your house, kill your wife and children and drag you off into slavery. But take heart, for in the long run they will be punished for their wicked deeds."

So Habakkuk complained again. He acknowledged the nation of Judah deserved to be punished, but he still didn't understand. A second time God answered his complaint with exactly the same answer He gave the first time. That should not surprise us, for God's answers are always constant. There is no turning with Him, no changes. His ways are absolute; it is man who must change—not God.

It was not until Habakkuk bent his knee before God in resignation, praying what Catherine Marshall calls the most powerful of all prayers, the prayer of relinquishment, that his complaints turned to a cry of victory. The heart of Habakkuk's book can be summed up in three progressive verses. He began with a statement of blind disgust:

For the vision is yet for an appointed time . . . the just shall live by his faith (Habakkuk 2:3–4).

He moved to a revelation:

For the earth shall be filled with the knowledge of the glory of the Lord, as the waters cover the sea (2:14).

And wound up with an exhortation of affirmation:

But the Lord is in his holy temple: let all the earth keep silence before him (2:20).

He then closes his book with a mighty prayer of resignation which G. Campbell Morgan once called "the greatest and most priceless passage in the whole of poetic prophecy":

Although the fig tree shall not blossom, neither shall fruit be in the vines; the labour of the olive shall fail, and the fields shall yield no meat; the flock shall be cut off from the fold, and there shall be no herd in the stalls: Yet I will rejoice in the Lord, I will joy in the God of my salvation. The Lord God is my strength, and he will make my feet like hinds' feet, and he will make me to walk upon mine high places (3:17–19).

That's looking at frogs and seeing princes. But before the transformation can take place, there is an awful lot of suffering. Any theology which denies suffering as a reality is incomplete and deals only on a superficial level, for suffering is God's greatest tool to accomplish His will. That's the reason God used Chaldeans to bring havoc on His chosen race, why He allowed the Jews and Romans to team up and crucify His Son, why He lets His people get spit on. It's all part of the training course designed by the Father and implemented by the Holy Spirit to bring us to the place of conformity to God's Son, Jesus Christ.

A former church musician called from Houston, asking if I would see him if he flew to Melbourne. I have a soft spot in my heart for men of God who have, for whatever reason, dropped out of the ministry. Beneath the froggy exterior I keep seeing the heart of a prince yearning to return to the service of the King. This man, at one time had been well-known among evangelical Chrisians. But there had been problems. Years ago while he was living in Memphis he had an affair with a single girl. She bore an illegitimate son. He loved her deeply, but because of his ministry—and because he already had a wife—he chose not to live with her.

The other woman took her child and moved to Houston where she went into the real estate business. The evangelist, on the other hand, tried to continue with his ministry. But there was no anointing of God. Things were not going well in his own house, even though they had, by then, a little baby of their own. His wife learned about his affair and was making life miserable. Finally, in desperation, the man left his wife and son and moved to Houston to be with his mistress.

But things were no better. By that time the illegitimate son had grown up and left home. He was part of the drug culture and rebellious toward all authority. He did not know the man who

195

had moved in with his mother was his real father and would not have cared had he known. The evangelist's wife, back in Tennessee, filed for divorce. She sold his beautiful grand piano and was threatening to get rid of all his other personal things. His state of misery finally became so acute that he called me from Houston, asking if he could fly over and talk.

I heard his sad story. The Chaldeans had stripped him clean The only point of contact left between him and God was his 11-year-old son back in Memphis, living with his wife. "I can walk away from my wife," he told me frankly. "I can walk away from my mistress. I can even walk away from God. But every time I put my head on my pillow, I think about that little curly-headed kid with the big glasses growing up back in Memphis without a daddy—and I can't stand it. I can't sleep. I can't eat. My heart is broken. All I can think about is that innocent child and all I have done to hurt him. Yet I cannot go back. My wife doesn't want me, and I don't want her. What can I do?"

He sat across from me, his head in his hands, his handsome face bathed in tears. Some say guilt is not of God. But guilt is of God if you're guilty. And this man was guilty. It was God who had brought him to this place of desperation.

"I have gone from preacher to preacher," he said. "They have listened to my story and every one of them has said, 'You need to become a Christian.'" He looked up at me. "But I am born again. There have been great moments in my life when I've loved God and tried to follow Him. I believe with all my heart I am a Christian. But all anyone can see is this horrible mess I am in. They see that I have walked away from my wife and child, that I am living with my mistress, that I have fathered a bastard, that I have left the church—and they say, 'Man, you need to accept Christ.'"

"Christians aren't immune from sin," I said frankly. "You're already a Christian. That's why you are so miserable. But an experience with Christ is not enough. You need the power of the Holy Spirit."

God doesn't say we move into sinless perfection the moment we are born again. True, our source of sin is cut off, but the human

196

nature remains, and we always live with the dregs. There is always the remnant of that old life, meaning we must constantly repent. I looked at the broken man in the chair. "It's not that you need a new salvation; you need to submit to the mighty hand of God that is at work in your life because you are a born-again person. How long can you rebel?"

I paused, then said matter-of-factly, "I will tell you the way out of your dilemma. All you have to do is to follow my advice, and your problem will be solved."

"Anything," he said with anxiety on his face. "I'll do anything just to be free."

"You must turn your back on both situations. You must turn your back on your mistress in Houston and never return to her. You must not even go back to pick up your belongings. Have her send them to you.

"Second, you must turn your back on your wife and your 11-year-old son. Give them up to God. Admit you have lost it all. Let your wife sell all your personal belongings. Let her go through with the divorce if that is what she wants. Relinquish all."

"But what will I do, then?" he asked.

"Oh, you'll stay right here. You can move in with some of our people, even with me if necessary, until you can find an apartment. Then you will get a job in this community. You will work with your hands at hard manual labor. You will be tightly surrounded by loving men and women who will help bring you to wholeness in this community setting. You are to remain here for one year. At the end of that time, all your problems will be solved, including the horrible situation between you and your young son."

"That's no answer," he said, his voice edged with anger.

"It's the only answer I have for you," I said gently.

"I thank you for your offer," he said in a stiff voice as he rose to his feet. "But you are asking the impossible."

"I don't think you understand what I'm offering," I said. "I am offering myself. I am opening my home and my life to take you in and steer you in the right direction—toward God."

"There must be an easier way," he said, starting to leave. "I'll just have to find it elsewhere."

197

"Listen to me," I said with as much sensitivity as I could. "If you do not obey willingly, then God will use force. He will do that because you are His child, because you are born again. He chastises those whom He loves. You think things are bad now; ask Him again and you'll get an even harder answer. Wait until your wife marries another man and your child is raised by someone who does not love him as a father—and all you can do about it is shiver in the night and weep. God loves you enough to rip your heart until you turn to Him."

Like the rich young ruler to whom Jesus said essentially the same thing, he turned away. The price was too great. And I could not go after him. Not that I did not want to, for I saw a beautiful prince beneath his froggy exterior—but I could only offer to kiss him. If he refused, as he did, there was nothing I could do. He walked out. I have not heard from him since.

In every man's life there are two gardens. One is like that garden from which man was exiled. It is the place where we once enjoyed all the beautiful things of God. There we felt alive. Creative. Filled with joy. In that garden, walking side by side with beautiful people, we felt fulfilled, exhilarated, satisfied. But we overstepped the invisible yet well-defined limitations. We tasted of forbidden fruit, feeling if fellowship was that good, how much better intimacy as well. Then, instead of repenting, we ran and hid—trying to justify our sin. So that Garden is now eternally closed. There stands at the gate an angel with a flaming sword, hiding the entrance behind his awfulness. Even the memories of those wonderful experiences are smudged and spoiled under the shame of our sin. To that garden there is no returning.

But in each man's life there is another garden—a little corner where precious things have been willfully buried. There is, on the back side of every lonely heart, a little private cemetery where we go, on occasion, to mourn and place flowers. Buried there are the things we have willfully—although reluctantly—banished from our lives. There, beneath the soil of obedience to God, lie buried priceless relationships, precious intimacies, loves dearer than life itself, things lawful yet not expedient. But in obedience we have put them aside. Using the spade of self-denial we have opened the ground to lay them tenderly beneath the sod. And although the grass has now covered the sites, the tombstones still recall the memories of deep earthly loves, the longings of our souls, even the dreams and desires of our hearts which we believed were given by God. Yet because of the time, or the tender circumstances, or the effect on gentle lambs, or simply the rightness of the act—we voluntarily turned our backs on the good in order to choose the best.

There is a difference between the two gardens. To the first we can never return. There we were discovered in our sin—and driven out. But we are given liberty to walk freely down the tender paths of the second garden, to listen to the echoes, to relive, if only in our hearts, the gentle moments of love and desire. For God is gracious to those who, as an act of obedience, bury the good beneath the soil of self-crucifixion—in order to await the resurrection of the best. For one day, when all the seeds of self are totally beneath the sod, there will come a cracking of the earth and a great resurrection of that which has been buried to His glory—rising in a glorified form.

Resurgam! I shall live again.

However, until that happens, the purposes of God may seem to be all darkness, rather than light.

Returning from a recent trip to the Sinai, our small group joined another tour group which had attended one of the World Conferences on the Holy Spirit sponsored by Logos International Fellowship. From Jerusalem we rode on huge tour buses to the Allenby Bridge across the Jordan River, then shifted to Arab buses to drive into Amman, Jordan, and on to the airport to catch our plane back to New York.

It was a strange transition, from our spartan and simple life in the desert to the bustling life of the tourist, riding in air-conditioned buses with people more concerned about their own personal needs than the needs of others. This was accented by the confusion at the Amman airport where we joined with almost 400 other people trying to force their way aboard a Royal Jordanian Airlines 747 jet. It was pandemonium. At the last moment the ticket agent for the airline had canceled all reserved seats and told the people they could sit anywhere they wanted. It was an every-man-for-himself situation as we tried to board the plane.

Nothing will bring out the carnal nature like a "you're-on-your-own" set of instructions. In particular, I was impressed with a middle-aged couple near us who had spent most of the day complaining that the meals were bad, the bus ride was bumpy, the tour guides discourteous and, in short, telling people they were disgusted and would never again come on such a tour. When the announcement was made that all seat assignments had been canceled and the people could sit wherever they wanted, the man grabbed his wife by her arm and with a curt, "Come on, Charlotte, let's go," started pushing his way through the crowd to the front of the line, determined to get the best seats themselves, regardless of who else got aboard.

Seeing their rude determination, many people simply stepped back and let them go ahead. All the glory of Israel and all the joy of the magnificent conference seemed to have been forgotten in the arrogance of this couple as they forced their way to the front of the line.

When the doors to the plane were finally opened, they went running down the aisle and picked the choice bulkhead seats so they could stretch their legs during the long overseas flight. As the other people boarded, they sat in their seats, looking straight ahead, a tiny smirk on their faces. If survival belonged to the fittest, they certainly qualified as fit for something.

The plane was almost full when I noticed my friend Dan Malachuk, who had sponsored the conference, helping his wife, Viola, up the stairs into the coach section. Viola had broken her foot in Israel and was hobbling painfully along, her leg encased in a huge plaster cast. All the good seats were gone, chosen long before by folks like the pushy couple who had rudely forced their way on first. Sensing that the Malachuks would have no place to sit, I got up from my seat in the rear of the plane and came forward to where the pushy couple were sitting.

"I hate to ask you to do this," I said, "but there is a lady with a broken foot coming aboard. She needs a seat where she can stretch her leg during the flight and prop it up."

I just stood there looking at the couple.

The man gave me an extremely mean look. "Are you suggesting we give them our seats?"

I just stood there, smiling. "There are a number of seats in the rear of the plane. You could be reasonably comfortable back there with the rest of us."

"You really mean it, don't you?" he sneered. "You have the gall to come up here and ask us to give up our good seats."

"Yes, sir," I said. "I really hate it. But this lady needs a place to prop her leg. Surely you could do that for the cause of Jesus."

"Well, I don't like it," he said. "I guess I don't have any choice. But this is the last time I'll ever come on any kind of trip with people like you."

Mumbling, grumbling, he got all his bags from under his seat and went back down the aisle to empty seats in the back. Viola had just arrived and tried to thank them, but they just brushed past her. She and Dan took their seats and with a moan of pain she stretched her leg so Dan could prop it up on her toilet case. I returned to my seat near my desert friends, feeling terrible.

Sitting down beside Mike Evans, who had been with me in the Sinai, I fidgeted. "Mike, I really feel bad about having to ask that couple to move. They've had such a hard time. Now they're back there cramped into seats not nearly as nice as the ones they had. I think I'll go back and try to comfort them."

Mike reached up and grabbed my arm. "God has been working on that couple ever since they've been on the tour," he said significantly. "Don't interrupt what the Holy Spirit is doing."

I sat back down in my seat. Mike was right. In my desire to be a peacemaker, I had let my soul begin to rule my spirit. Here was a couple, a man and wife, who someplace along the line had committed themselves to the lordship of Jesus Christ. Now God was using some extremely rough circumstances to smooth their sharp edges. It would be unwise for me to pour oil on water which God had troubled.

Just before we took off, someone in the first class section came back and arranged for the Malachuks to move to the front of the plane, where the seats were wider and there was plenty of room to stretch out. When they did, the grumpy couple was able to return to their original seats at the bulkhead. But they remained angry all the way across the ocean. However, I agree with Mike that it was probably the most memorable plane ride they ever had, for the Holy Spirit was obviously at work in the lives of two Kingdom frogs.

Affliction, chastisement, hardship, suffering—all are God's means to bring us to the place of obedience, to bring us to the place of the Spirit-controlled life. Why be satisfied with a lily pad, when a throne awaits your call?

XII

Riding the Wind

As long as I can remember there has been locked in my heart the desire to do daring things, to risk my life, so to speak, in adventure. But fear had locked the door on my venturing spirit—fear, and self-imposed circumstances. The only times I dared step out were to do clandestine things which only temporarily satisfied that driving desire to achieve, create, risk, and dare. At the same time, though, I continued to yearn for a legitimate expression to that longing, some way to unlock the door of the cage of my soul so my spirit could soar like the eagle.

Some men find their outlet in the world of business—risking great sums of money for the thrill of gain. Others turn to athletics, disciplining their bodies so they may risk all on the high diving board, by pitting themselves against a brawny opponent or defying death by scaling some challenging mountain peak. Others satisfy their drive for adventure by defying the world to discover them as they move from one tryst to another, planning ingenious ways to meet their lover in a forlorn rendezvous. Most, however, are forced to satisfy their spirit of adventure vicariously. This accounts, in the main, for the tremendous popularity of adventure movies, spy novels, western sagas on television and even pornographic literature and films. All provide a measure of vicarious release to the chained spirit of adventure which beats its wings on the bars of the cages of the soul. Or, like Thurber's Walter Mitty, we develop our own secret life of fantasy. We lie awake at night imagining we are not really a middle-aged grocer, a computer technician or even the pastor of a church. Rather, putting aside the reality of a slumbering wife in our subdivision bedroom, we become, during those last moments of waking consciousness, a renowned brain surgeon, a dashing fighter pilot or a deep sea diver on a mission of mercy to rescue helpless sailors from a disabled submarine. However, by liberating our fantasies and imaginations, we only feed crumbs to the eagle of our spirit, rather than allowing him to do what he yearns to do—soar free on the thermal currents of God, venturing forth through the tough places.

In my own desperate attempts to free my spirit for that for which I had been born, I ran the gauntlet of all these escapes—and many more. In each of them I found a taste of reality, but it was never lasting—or satisfying. Like a runaway boy, drifting down a river on a raft, I began to catch a whiff of salt air and hear the roar of the surf. But I could in no way comprehend the immensity of what God had in store for me as I rounded the next bend and came face to face with who I was created to be.

Jesus said that when the Holy Spirit comes into our lives He will lead us to all truth. Receiving Him is the greatest of all adventures. He is the key which unlocks the door of our inner being and allows our own spirit, that part of us breathed into us by the Father, to soar free—liberated.

The baptism in the Holy Spirit, though glorious, is also fraught with danger and risk. No longer will we ever be satisfied to feed our own spirit crumbs of fantasy and imagination. Having tasted the reality of God, we will be compelled to move upward, escaping the bonds of our carnal nature and taking on, more and more, the adventurous, daring attributes of God's Son—who was the greatest explorer and adventurer of all. For those few who are willing to risk all, to venture out, to die to self, there are precious and unique blessings ahead which the less venturesome will never experience. Such blessings cannot be transmitted, only experienced; they are existential, not visionary; they cannot be given away, only enjoyed at the moment. Such experiences—and there will be innumerable ones for the Spirit-controlled individual—are like those fragile yet exquisite wild flowers sometimes found on the windswept pinnacle of the mountain. You stoop and examine, enjoy and are blessed by their symmetry, elegance and loveliness. How splendid is their form, how delicate their petals, how brilliant their color. The next day you return with a loved one, but the flowers are gone. They lasted but a day, and only the ones present at the hour they blossomed could experience and enjoy. They are God's gift to those who dare venture out.

I close this book by telling you three little stories which illustrate how the Holy Spirit has activated my own spirit of adventure. He has unlocked the cage of my soul and allowed the eagle to ride the winds to the tops of mountains where I have tasted nectar I once thought reserved for God alone. I no longer have to fantasize, to daydream at my desk or sit in the evening staring at the fire, imagining romantic things. Since that grand unlocking a dozen years ago, life has been one continuing adventure. Those close to me are aware of my occasional slips back into carnality. But despite this, I know something special has happened to me. And that's the reason I want to share these little stories, stories of times when the eagle of my spirit caught the upward surge of God's thermals and allowed me to brush my feathers across the face of God.

The first took place on one of my research trips into the Sinai. During our last night in the desert we pulled our vehicle into a hidden canyon next to a unique, sandswept grotto. Hollowed out of the side of the wadi, gouged by the fingers of the wind from thousands of years of shaping, was a natural chapel. That evening after supper, two of the men placed candles in some of the hundreds of little sockets which had been carved by the wind from the red sandstone sides of the open-topped cave, hollow sockets behind a breathtaking façade of red and purple stone. Then, sitting on the soft sand, we waited as the brief twilight turned into darkness. In the dancing shadows of the flickering candlelight which played across the sand and brushed the faces of the men sitting quietly around the grotto—we listened.

At first all we could hear was the gentle sound of the dying wind as it swished and moaned through the rocks. Then, as darkness enveloped us and the Sinai stars appeared overhead in all their brilliance, all we could hear was our own breathing, and the gentle beating of a dozen hearts beside us.

Someone quoted a passage from the Psalms:

Before the mountains were brought forth, or ever thou hadst formed the earth and the world, even from everlasting to everlasting, thou art God . . .

Someone else prayed a soft prayer of thanksgiving and praise Someone else began to sing:

Praise the name of Jesus,
    He's my Rock, He's my Fortress .

We joined in and then let our voices follow the focus of our hearts as our singing departed from the confines of structure and soared gently into the Spirit, listening, at the same time, as the angels of the Sinai—those special heavenly beings who live in that desolate section of the world—joined in. How seldom do they have a chance in that forsaken wilderness to blend their voices with those of the redeemed.

Then, as the evening grew quiet—with a stillness not equaled anyplace else on earth—one of the men, Derrel Emmerson, began to sing alone. I listened intently, for it was a new song. It was beautiful, a quiet chorus of praise which I assumed Derrel had often sung in his church back in the Washington, D.C., area. He sang three stanzas, repeating the chorus between each stanza. I wished I had brought my little tape recorder into the grotto so I could have captured the song. I made a mental note to ask him to sing it into my recorder the next day. I wanted to learn it so I could take it back and teach it to my friends in Florida.

The next morning as we were breaking camp to head northward, I took my little tape recorder out of my duffel bag, found Derrel where he was rolling up his sleeping bag and asked if he would repeat the song he sang last night.

"What song?" Derrel asked.

"The one you sang in the grotto," I answered. "That beautiful little chorus your folks must sing in your church."

Derrel grinned. "I don't remember it."

"I don't understand. You sang all three stanzas last night. I can almost remember it myself but not quite."

"I'm sorry," he laughed, returning to his packing in the sand. "But I was singing in the Spirit. It was all spontaneous."

"But it had perfect rhyme and meter. You repeated the chorus with each stanza."

"I know," he said. "But it was just one of those very special times. I sensed the presence of the angels around me, and suddenly I was singing. Perhaps it was only for their ears, since they don't have much company down here. Whatever, it was obviously not meant to be repeated—for I cannot remember a single line of the lyrics or melody."

There are special blessings, I've learned, awaiting those who venture out. Authored in eternity, they break through into time and space only as men move upward toward God. They are never to be repeated, never to be shared, never to be wrapped in a package to be given away. They are like the blessings of breath: inhaled deeply, disseminated into the system and never to be recovered in form, only in energy. Each step of the way He guides, leading us to new heights of adventure and experience. The way may seem dangerous as we turn loose of all the safety devices of the past and set our faces toward the things of the Spirit, but there is a glorious reward far more precious than the turquoise nuggets of the ancient mines which awaits those who dare run the risk of discovery.

The joy of adventure remains only as long as God controls. When man steps in with his reasons and fears to institutionalize and structure (or even record) that which is meant to flow free and unencumbered, life leaves. Yet it is this lack of institutionalizing which is the single factor preventing us from venturing out. How desperately the human soul wants to see a blueprint of the next step, to exert an element of control over what is about to happen. That is only our own humanity, which is afraid of the unknown, not that essence of God inside each of us. It is the essence of God which urges us to dare, to release our tow line to that mechanical device which has helped us break the elementary bonds of earth, and soar free on Zephyr's currents toward the dwelling place of the Most High.

After that final night in the wilderness, our small group of men packed our gear and boarded our open truck for the long ride back to Jerusalem. Driving eastward through the expanding valleys we hit the coastal road along the Gulf of Elat and drove north through the deep, geographical rift called the "Arabah" to the western coast of the Dead Sea. The west wind blowing off the Negev Desert was oven temperature, and by the time we reached the beautiful oasis at Ein Gedi we were almost parched.

Ein Gedi is a deep ravine almost two miles long. References to it appear throughout the Bible. It was here David encountered Saul and had the opportunity to slay him while he was alone in one of the numerous caves along the valley. Instead, he only cut a piece of cloth from Saul's garment and told his lieutenants that he could not "touch God's anointed." It was also here that David wrote some of his most beautiful psalms. The valley still abounds with wild life, mountain sheep, ibex and smaller rodents.

The Hebrew word "ein" means "spring." And at the top of the deep ravine is a magnificent waterfall, flowing from this huge spring. Below are a series of smaller waterfalls and deep pools of clear, running water. The stream eventually spills into the Dead Sea, 1,200 feet below sea level. While the rest of the men went ahead to the waterfall at the top of the ravine, three of us—Mike Evans, Derrel Emmerson and I—stopped to swim in a secluded pool formed from solid rock. I had been to the top before, and after the hot dusty ride climaxing two weeks in the desert, I was ready for a cool dip in pure water.

We stripped, laid our shorts and sandals on a high rock near the water and plunged into the icy pool. For days our skin had been parching in the sun, and the sensation of the cool water swirling around our bodies as we splashed and frolicked was delightful. In the shallow places we could rest on the cool rocks, letting the water caress our skin and enjoying the sun which filtered through the overhanging trees and danced like diamonds on the surface.

After long minutes of immersing our bodies in the water, we crawled up on a huge warm boulder. The other men in our group had scattered up and down the canyon. Yet we knew, all three of us in a corporate way, we were not alone in that quiet, secluded place. Others had been there before us: David the shepherd, the mighty warrior Joab, the prophet Samuel. Their spirits had left an indelible presence in the canyon. But it was not this "communion of the saints" which attracted us nor even again the presence of angels as much as our deep awareness of the presence of the Holy Spirit.

In an act of simple worship, the three of us stood, stark naked, our bare feet on the warm surface of the rock, and raised our hands toward heaven. The sun broke through the trees and bathed us in warmth, drying our wet bodies as we stood, voicing our praise to God in word and "spiritual song," singing in the spirit and shouting praises which echoed back and forth off the steep rock walls of the wadi. It was a special moment of high ecstasy, rapturous in nature, as we presented our bodies before Jehovah God.

Free from all inhibitions, released from embarrassment, liberated from the restraints of culture and clothes, I began to soar. Ecstasy, in this case, cannot be equated with the popular and cheapened sense of "hysteria" but goes far deeper to the historical, etymological sense of "ex-stasis"—that is, literally to "stand out from," to be freed from the perpetual dichotomy of most human activity until there is but one focus—God. *Ecstasy* is the accurate term for the intensity of consciousness that occurs in pure worship. It is far more than the Bacchic concept of "letting go"; it involves the total person—body, soul, and spirit—subconscious acting in unity with the conscious—intellect, emotion and spirit joining in one intense concentration on God. Not before, nor since, have I felt as totally immersed in the *ecstasy* of worship—soaring with the eagles.

The third and final adventure story I want to tell has to do with the lesson I learned from my father shortly after I returned from that particular trip to the Sinai. Watching my dad grow old was one of the great experiences of my life. My father was my hero. I admired everything he did. I admired the way he quoted long passages of Kipling, Longfellow and James Whitcomb Riley. When I was a child I respected him as a man of ethics and nobility, a churchman in the cultural sense of the word. Later, after he surrendered his life to Jesus Christ in his 60th year, I respected him even more as a committed Christian. I was impressed with his business ability. I honored his financial wisdom. But most of all, I respected him as a man. Although his world, during those last few years of his life, was confined to his wheelchair, his desk and his bed, nevertheless he remained a great adventurer. Always exploring. Always venturing out in his mind and spirit.

On his 80th birthday he began to grow a mustache. He had always been clean shaven, but the closer he grew to eternity, the more he let his inhibitions and traditions fall away.

"I've wanted to grow a mustache since I started shaving, 67 years ago," he said. "But it was never proper in my circles. Now I am putting away many of my proper things and becoming real."

He wore it for five years and shaved it off. "It's just not me," he said. "But I'm glad I did it just the same."

I loved him for it. And I loved him for the other areas of adventure I recognized in his life. We had always been a very "proper" family. But in his later years, Daddy finally found freedom to put his arms around women other than his beloved wife of more than 50 years. The older he grew, he told me, the more he realized he had confused impropriety with impurity. Life was too short not to enjoy all the beautiful things God had put around him.

When we prayed together, as we often did when I visited him, he would defy his old Methodist tradition and join in with a hearty "Amen!" or a sincere "Praise the Lord!" Sometimes he would sit in his wheelchair and raise his hands in worship as I read to him or as one of his women friends played the piano and sang. He was not ashamed when others saw him weep when he was moved emotionally. And he loved to take my mother's hand or kiss her in front of the children and grandchildren, something we had never seen him do in his younger years. Some may have equated his "freedom" with senility or old age; I attributed it to spiritual maturity.

Thus, as he approached the time of dying, I watched him closely.

Of all the things I wanted to learn from him, how to approach death was the most important. I have often contrasted my reaction to my father's preparation to die with that of the contemporary poet, Dylan Thomas. Thomas, writing on the death of his father, you remember, began his poem by saying:

> Do not go gentle into that good night,
> Old age should burn and rave at the close of day;
> Rage, rage against the dying of the light.

And the poem ends:

> And you, my father, there on the sad height,
> Curse, bless me now with your fierce tears, I pray.
> Do not go gentle into that good night.
> Rage rage against the dying of the light.

Of course it was the son writing, not the father. The father had to confront death and in some way accept it. But he did it battling against the insurgent spirit of the son, who, despite the piercing elegance of the poem, was still rebelling against a God who would take from him the man who meant most in his life.

On the other hand, I never, not once, had any desire to ask my father to linger or to plead with him to rage against his appointment with death. Indeed, I urged him to go gentle into that good night and to bless me, not with fierce tears, but to bless me with insights into eternity—and to communicate, as much as was humanly possible, all he learned as he walked through the valley of the shadow.

My father saw old age as the greatest of all the adventures of life. His ongoing prayer was that as his body wore out, he would remain alert in mind so he could savor and enjoy all that lay ahead. My father never drank alcohol—not a drop that I know of. Alcohol was a depressant, he said, and he wanted to remain alert with every cell of his body to experience all that God had for him as he ascended the heights. Nor did he need it, as some do, to free him from his inhibitions. In his later years he found the stimulant of the Holy Spirit was all that was necessary to give him the upsurge of vitality necessary to sense and enjoy the experiences of life.

Yet as I watched my father—moving rapidly toward eternity—become free, I realized how stiff and unyielding I remained in many areas of my life. Especially was this true in my expression of affection between us. Our family had never been overtly affectionate. We seldom hugged and almost never kissed—at least not when I was a boy. Occasionally my mother would kiss me, but I had never, to my knowledge, kissed my daddy. We men shook hands. Daddy taught us how to give a firm, manly handshake and how to look the other fellow straight in the eye while we were doing it. But as I watched him become free and felt my own love for him growing, I longed to express my affection in a more physical way. Yet every time I was with him and it came time to say goodby, instead of bending and kissing him as he sat in his wheelchair, I always stuck out my hand. Even the words "I love you" stuck in my throat. Like taking off my clothes at Ein Gedi, it was something I wanted to do—but was afraid to try.

Finally I could stand it no longer. My sophistication and my twisted concepts of masculinity were choking me to death. One Saturday afternoon I got in the car and made a special trip south along the Florida coast to my parents' home, 35 miles away. Walking into my dad's little study, I found him in his wheelchair, at work on his ledger.

"I have come for one purpose," I said. "I want to tell you something and then I want to do something."

He looked up, grinned, and said, "Fine."

Suddenly I felt like a fool. I was 46 years old—he was 86. But I had come this far and was not going to back out.

"I love you," I said, choking up.

"Is that what you came to tell me?" he asked gently, putting his pen on the desk beside his green ledger and resting his hands in his lap.

"Yes, sir," I said.

"You didn't have to come all the way down here to tell me that," he grinned. Then he added, "But I'm sure glad you did."

"I've wanted to voice the words with my lips for years," I said.

212

"I find it easy to write them on paper. And I know you have known. But it has been difficult for me to say it with my mouth. Perhaps," I added, "I needed to say it more for me than for you."

His face grew pensive, and he nodded slowly.

"There is something else," I said.

He did not look up from his place at the desk but continued to look straight ahead, nodding slowly.

I bent and kissed him, first on one cheek, then the other, then on top of his bald forehead.

He reached up, took my arms in his strong hands, and pulled me down to him so he could put his arms around my neck. For long moments we remained in that awkward position—me bending over his wheelchair, he with his arms around my neck, pulling my face up against his. Finally he released me, and I straightened up. There was a trace of tears in his eyes, and his lip quivered as he spoke.

"My father died when I was a young man back in Indiana," he said. "I left home shortly afterwards to go to college, teach school and finally go to France in World War I. After the war I moved to Florida. I never returned home except for occasional visits to see my mother.

"When my mother grew old, I invited her to come live with us." He paused, and his face broke into one of those knowing grins. "Guess what she said? She said, 'No, I'll stay right on here in Morristown in this house. But I love you for asking me to come live with you and even though I'll never do it, I hope you keep right on asking me up until the day I die.'"

Looking up at me, he added, his lip quivering again, "I know you love me. But I hope you keep right on telling me—up until the day I die."

Something broke loose in me that Saturday afternoon. Something which had been knotted up for years. Once again, as I had in the Sinai, I felt my spirit burst free. I left my parents' house in Vero Beach wanting to run home, leaping and dancing, rather than getting in the car and driving back up the coast. My wings, like the eagle's, were locked against the storm. I was soaring.

Dr. J. Wilbur Chapman is reported to have asked General William Booth, the founder of the Salvation Army, what was the secret of his success. Booth replied, "I will tell you the secret. God has had all there was of me."

I'm not there yet, but I'm a lot closer than I have ever been. That's why I have written this book. It's all tied in with my own purpose in life—my defined reason for existence. I wrote it to encourage you to release yourself to the control of the Holy Spirit, to dare to cross mine fields, to climb mountains, to explore caves, to hear the voice from behind the ranges. I have written to urge you to attempt the impossible, to run the risk of failure, to dare to praise, to dare to love, to dare to die to self. I have written in hopes you will become the person you are—which is the essence of salvation—and to know the joy, the thrill, of letting the Holy Spirit control your life as you soar like the eagle through the tough ventures of life.

A Way Through the Wilderness

by Jamie Buckingham

Jamie Buckingham has ventured through the wilderness of Sinai on many occasions, following in the footsteps of the children of Israel.

He has also known the tortuous route of spiritual pilgrimage, through failure and a sense of uselessness to joyful restoration by the ministering of the Holy Spirit. Carefully and beautifully he combines his personal experience with the lessons of the wilderness, sharing the simple truths of God's grace and faithfulness first revealed to Moses.

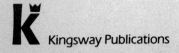
Kingsway Publications

Risky Living
Keys to Inner Healing

by Jamie Buckingham

Have we grown comfortable, finding it easier to wear a mask than to permit God to expose us – and change us?

This book is about the risks and rewards of opening ourselves to the refining work of the Holy Spirit. 'God knows I'm not there yet,' says Jamie Buckingham. 'The other day I argued with my wife and because she refused to do the brash things I suggested, I stormed out and called her a "stick in the mud".'

The author is deeply honest – and helpful. 'One of the most important keys to inner healing', he says, 'is praying in the Spirit.' And we all need the inner healing of fear and hurts before we can take the risk of living openly with ourselves, with God, and with one another.

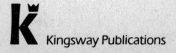

Kingsway Publications

Miracle Power

by Jamie Buckingham

There are no limits to what God may choose to do to - and through - us.

'Miracles should be the norm in the life of the Christian', insists Jamie Buckingham. 'Because we are constantly stumbling through a dark world, we need God to guide our footsteps, giving us the ability to walk supernaturally.

'That means miracles. But God is not restoring miracles to the church. They've been there all along. He is simply waiting for simple people who will step forward in faith and expect God to use them.'

Jamie Buckingham has experienced many miracles himself in the course of his long ministry. His study of miracles in the New Testament and today - miracles of healing, power, provision and hope - is designed 'to stimulate you, excite you and hopefully to convince you that the miracles of Jesus were not for yesterday - they are for today.'

Jamie Buckingham is the author of many books including *Risky Living*, *Where Eagles Soar* and *The Truth Will Set You Free, But First It Will Make You Miserable*.

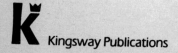

Kingsway Publications

The Nazarene

by Jamie Buckingham

A face-to-face encounter with the Messiah.

While exploring the Holy Land, Jamie Buckingham made a
number of trips into the Sinai. 'The more I visited,' he
relates, 'the more I developed a love not only for the people
who live there today, but for the land itself—the land of
the Bible. Eventually I began simply to follow the footsteps
of Jesus through the Holy Land. I had become—and
remain—consumed by this man called the Nazarene.'

Walk where Jesus walked. Travel with him through the
desert's sweltering heat; stand with him on the windswept
shores of Galilee; feel with him the excitement of the
crowds and the astonishment of the disciples.

Experience, in this collection of sharply-focused
meditations, the presence of the Nazarene.

'Leads us to deeper insights into history—and a deeper
love for Jesus.'

—JACK HAYFORD

Jamie Buckingham is the author of numerous books, including
Miracle Power.

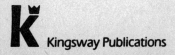

Kingsway Publications

The Truth Will Set You Free...

by Jamie Buckingham

No-one escapes the pointed pen of Jamie Buckingham.

Renowned storyteller (even his wife says most of his stories are true) and master satirist, Jamie goes behind the scenes to find targets for his wit and wry observations. Big shots, his friends and family, particularly himself—all are pilloried in this hilarious collection.

Through it all Jamie's keen sense of the ludicrous throws his faith into sharper relief. This book will make you laugh. It may also nudge you a little bit closer to God.

'You ought to try to live with him.'

—Jamie's wife

'If he says another word about my hair transplant, he's fired.'

—One of his publishers

JAMIE BUCKINGHAM is a pastor in Florida and author of many books including *Risky Living*, *A Way Through the Wilderness* and *Where Eagles Soar*.

Minstrel
Published by Kingsway

The Hot Line

by Peter H. Lawrence

'This is the beginner's book written by a beginner for beginners,' says Peter Lawrence. 'It is a veritable collection of signs and blunders, with laughter one minute and tears the next...God loves some decidedly odd people. This book is written by one of them.'

Many Christians today are willing to accept that God does speak to people. However, it is often difficult to discern the voice of God.

From his own experience over the past fifteen years Peter Lawrence offers guidance on the costly but enthralling path of obedience to God. 'Learning to recognise, receive, test and give "words" from God is just like learning any other discipline. There are no easy answers and there is no cheap grace.'

'Superbly written. It is humorous, self-deprecating, profoundly honest (especially about failure) and intensely readable...Remember that the same God is your God and can do as much through you.'

Michael Green

THE REV PETER LAWRENCE has been Vicar of Christ Church, Burney Lane, Birmingham since 1979. He and his wife Carol have three daughters. He is a keen sportsman and former English teacher.

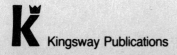
Kingsway Publications

Only Love Can Make A Miracle

by Mahesh Chavda

'Suddenly I became aware of a brilliant white light coming towards me. I turned and saw a man walking towards me. I knew immediately who it was. It was Jesus.'

Mahesh Chavda grew up in Mombassa, Kenya, the son of a prominent Hindu teacher. He grew disillusioned and turned to the Bible. One night God spoke to him in a powerful vision, and he gave his life to Christ.

As a graduate student in Texas, he was gripped by the power of the Spirit. Almost despite himself an extraordinary ministry developed: travelling worldwide he would be used by God to cast out evil spirits, raise the dead, give sight to the blind and lead thousands and thousands to Christ. This ministry among the world's poor continues today.

'Through this testimony , God can encourage your faith.'
—COLIN URQUHART

'What a revelation of humility, faith, love and power! Mahesh's amazing story reveals the inner motivations of a man who has overcome huge disappointments and scaled the heights of faith with astonishing results. This book is a must for anyone who wants to be stimulated to grow in their knowledge of God and to serve him more powerfully.'

—TERRY VIRGO

Illustrated with 14 pages of remarkable photographs.

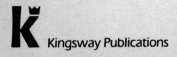

Kingsway Publications

Nine O'Clock in the Morning

by Dennis J. Bennett

How could a successful Rector of a 2,500 strong congregation risk the future of his ministry and the unity of the church by getting involved with the 'baptism in the Spirit', 'speaking in tongues', and all that?

And how could the same man take over a run-down mission church and see it renewed by the Spirit into one of the most spiritually alive churches in North America?

The marks of the Spirit's presence have always been the same: a new reality of God, a love for Jesus Christ, a hunger for the Scriptures, spontaneous joy and praise and witness, generous giving...

Dennis Bennett's fascinating account will undoubtedly stimulate faith in the lives of many readers.

David Watson

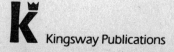
Kingsway Publications

The Holy Spirit and You

by Dennis and Rita Bennett

The author of *Nine o'clock in the morning* and his wife write on the day-to-day application of a supernatural Christianity. Millions of Christians, both ordained and lay, have received the Holy Spirit as at Pentecost, but relatively few succeed in finding instruction and advice on how to live their lives in the light and power of this experience. This book will answer a real need for many people.

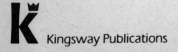